FIGURING OUT ROMAN NOBILITY

EXETER STUDIES IN HISTORY

General Editors:
Jonathan Barry, Tim Rees *and* T.P. Wiseman

Other paperbacks in this series include:

Roman Political Life, 90 BC–AD 69
edited by T.P. Wiseman (1985)

The Administration of the Roman Empire, 241 BC–AD 193
edited by David Braund (1988)

Satire and Society in Ancient Rome
edited by Susan H. Braund (1989)

Flavius Josephus: *Death of an Emperor*
translated with an Introduction and Commentary
by T.P. Wiseman (1991)

Historiography and Imagination, Eight Essays on Roman Culture
T.P. Wiseman (1994)

Roman Public Buildings
edited by Ian M. Barton (new edition 1995)

Roman Domestic Buildings
edited by Ian M. Barton (1996)

Phlegon of Tralles' Book of Marvels
translated with an Introduction and Commentary
by William Hansen (1996)

FIGURING OUT ROMAN NOBILITY

Juvenal's Eighth *Satire*

John Henderson

UNIVERSITY
of
EXETER
PRESS

First published in 1997 by
University of Exeter Press
Reed Hall, Streatham Drive
Exeter, Devon EX4 4QR
UK

British Library Cataloguing in Publication Data
A catalogue record for this book
is available from the British Library

ISBN 0 85989 517 3

Typeset in Monotype Sabon by
Michael Mepham, Frome, Somerset

Printed and bound in Great Britain by
Cromwell Press, Broughton Gifford, Wiltshire

CONTENTS

Preface   vii

Introduction: which of your relatives need you to exist?   1

1   On the way in: text and translation of Juvenal, *Satire* 8. 1–38   5

2   *Noblesse oblige*: what are pedigrees?   9

3   Rome in the *nomen*: naming in Latin   14

4   Pedigree chums: the poetics and politics of Roman names   22

5   It's no good calling people names: vv. 1–5   25

6   *Canst thou not remember Quintius, Fabricius, Curius, Regulus?* : the 'generalizing plural' in Latin   29

7   Why the little boy was glad that everyone called him Cyril: v. 3   33

8   Curiouser and Curioser: v. 4   37

9   Fallen idols: vv. 4–5   39

10   The fame of the name: vv. 6–9   42

11   That for a game of soldiers: vv. 9–12   48

12   Absolutely Fabius: vv. 13–8   50

13   *Courage, mon brave*: vv. 19–20   60

CONTENTS

14 Lloyd's names: vv. 21–38   64

15 All the way, allways: translation of Juvenal, *Satire* 8.
    39–275   73

16 Off you go and make a name for yourself: vv. 39–275   84

17 On your way out, if you wouldn't mind . . . : Juvenal,
    Satires, Book 3   94

Appendix 1. Horace, *Odes* 1. 12 and the 'generalizing
    plural': discussion (with text and translation)   97
Appendix 2. Virgil's roll-call of Roman *Exempla*: *Aeneid*
    6. 808–86, synopsis, text and translation   115
Appendix 3. Fabius Maximus in Virgil, Livy, Ovid:
    discussion (with texts and translations)   123
Appendix 4. Glossary of Roman *cognomina*: why is a
    Roman Emperor like P?   131

Notes   133
Bibliography: works referred to in the text and notes   163
Index: chief passages discussed in the text and notes   167

PREFACE

My experience is that people who read prefaces don't read the book, so I'll say briefly here what you're about to miss. This is a shortish book that (probably) grew out of a long-standing dialogue with Susanna Morton Braund, who has done most to show how good Juvenal's *Satires* are *after* his first two books.[1] *Satire* 8, on Roman 'nobility', is given a different twist in my account. In the first place, I treat the poem as a pure performance text. This is to say that I am not looking, as other interpreters have, for any expressive declaration from the author. I shan't identify a moralistic or a nihilistic speaker, for example. Rather, I see such identifications as ways to 'produce' the script. I aim to defer premature closure, whether in the name of the author or of a *persona* (mask, or character) constructed by the writing, not least because these brands of critical position have both been associated with depoliticizing criticism, all too persuasively and prevalently. I shall hold out for a succession of partly-open rhetorical positions of utterance which oblige performers of the text to invest and so commit (betray, image, figure) themselves in their readings. The moment of impersonation will be the juncture where closure is, at each reading, performatively effected. To sloganize: such are, in my simplistic version, the poetics and politics of difference. The subtext is that I do not see any harm in enjoying this poem *for all you are worth*. But I warn you that you'll have to face up to the corollary, that you have precious little choice about what that amounts to—and some of us *must* have a nasty surprise in store.

The reason why I think Juvenal figuring out Roman nobility will reward your attention is that his powerful and sustained tirade holds up a tangle of key processes of Roman sociality for ghoulish and gleeful, or, it may be, rancorous and outraged, mauling. The sanctity, the money, and (inevitably) the *sanctimoney*, of the grand old family names that had been immortalized by all the institutions of the fame-factory of the world-conquering Empire make for a topic that tweaks the entire ensemble of cultural tokens through which were negotiated, thought and lived education, ambition, regulation, validation and recognition. Juvenal studs his poem with an array of great names that put in play our competence in the traditional encyclopedia of *exempla* (symbolic figures caught in emblematic vignettes), and so our sense of Roman historicality. At the same time, Juvenal's citations are references to the classic antecedents in poetry who showcased and immortalized such *exempla*, and so they tilt at our *literary* reading-competence. By Juvenal's day, the Latin library was well-stocked with poetry, with canonical Virgil, Horace and Ovid, but also (in particular) with an adventurous *stemma* (family tree) of strident epics, from Manilius, through Lucan, Statius, and Silius. The declamatory rhetoric of Juvenal pushes this literary domain toward disclosing its emplotment in the generation of Roman culture. Intimacy with prestige poetry did much to engender Romanness, in terms of enhancing and stigmatizing patterns of behaviour and principles for living; but also, not least, in terms of providing an arena for contesting style, swagger and sense of humour.

Roman Verse Satire veers about between high-flown diction and well-squeezed poeticism at one moment, and impertinent colloquialism and sordid slang the next. So do I. Toward the end of this book, you may find I begin to enjoy the idea that Juvenal comes out and mocks his readers all too much, and start joining in. Any bad lass or lad who skips straight to the end will (I promise) instantly have cause to regret it. I do know that we aren't exactly used to 'textbooks' playing performative in this way; but I think that's why few writers get across how manipulatively alive so many classical texts really are. That's the point, as I see it: I hope my excesses may be a provocation. So, get your flip to the back out of the way, and then start in on Juvenal's poem along with me. And if you do any of this, you'll have the satisfaction of proving the first thing I said here to be wrong.

All dates are BCE unless otherwise indicated.

INTRODUCTION

WHICH OF YOUR RELATIVES
NEED YOU TO EXIST?[2]

1 THE GUIDED TOUR

Before stepping inside Juvenal, *Satire* 8, I shall try to unpack what the
poet sets himself to explore under the rubric of 'The Aristocracy'
(Chapter 2), and usher in a guide to the cultural poetics of Roman
nomenclature (Chapter 3). This pair of discussions prepares the way
for a presentation of the subject of Roman pedigrees as the grand
'problem' that this fierce poem of Juvenal digs over, while he gets on
with burying their dignity. Between his Roman crests, coats of arms and
mottoes, the stern satirist writes a drawing-room full of traditional
poetic uplift, into a dazzling overload of post-classical rhetoric.

   In this study, we shall be proceeding carefully through the exhibits
in Juvenal's opening sally, which parades a salon stuffed with famous
old names hallowed in the Roman tradition. The barrage serves to quiz,
engage and soften up the reader, with *Scipiones*, *Fabii*, and the rest of
the heroic names (vv. 1–18; Chapters 4–12). This prepares us for the
apophthegm (pithy slogan) in which Juvenal's own answer to the
problem is condensed (vv. 19–20; Chapter 13). He explores his *bon
mot* in the protreptic (animating exhortation) he at once delivers. This
is to be Juvenal's lesson, as he tells us what to do with ourselves, in no
uncertain terms (vv. 21–38; Chapter 14).

Finally, I shall show, in a much swifter sketch, how the rest of the poem reaches out to engross the ambitions and aspirations of every budding Roman (vv. 39–275; Chapter 16); and how the poem sits with its predecessor and successor, the other compositions in Juvenal's third *Book*—in a class of its own (Chapter 17). Juvenal's virtuoso writing deserves sustained close reading, for it tackles a series of concerns, with culture, career, and sexuality, that bring readers straight to what Romans were all about. I shall scrutinize the big names strewn through the length of the poem.

The lion's share of this study, however, goes to the proem of the central *Satire* 8, which obliges readers to bore right into the system of conceptual images through which Roman reality, not just their names, was negotiated, imposed and contested. The multitude of pieces of cultural knowledge on display in this poem's lobby (not all of them sins and sinners) does duty for a Roman guide to Rome. Perhaps *the* guide, but, at the least, a critical guide well aware of the competition, and out to rough them up a little. You can find out plenty from the way Juvenal handles the opportunity he saw in the subject of *stemmata* (family trees). Sparks fly when the satirist gets to work.

You'll find a text and translation of the proem (vv. 1–38; Chapter 1) immediately after this brief Introduction (pp. 5–8); and, in its proper place, a translation of the body of the poem (pp. 73–83; Chapter 15). For reference purposes, the end papers include a Glossary of Roman *cognomina* (nicknames) that have featured in the text, together with meanings attributed to them (pp. 131–2); and an Index of the Chief Passages discussed in the text and notes (pp. 167–8).

2 FAMILY AND FAME

There was no other way. However far afield, across the length and breadth of the imperial World State, fame at Rome had to be won on forays that all began by passing out into the world through the main hall of a family's house or palace, with its pile of ancestral honours and decorations. The Roman élite meant to keep it that way, too. Juvenal rubs in how determined both Roman education and reading culture

2

were to engrain in boys the imperative to live up to their heritage, and shoulder the onus of all this symbolic capital. Epic poetry, in particular, was the textual vector for this drive to condition the future. Thus Juvenal's quasi-epic *Satire* mocks poems that do what it does; but its mockery is at the same time itself another way to inculcate the old lessons, however silly and quaint it shows them to have been all along. Mockery attends celebrity: the great clans knew to keep infamy in the family.

3 LITERARY ANCESTRY

Juvenal's poem is the strong work of a major classic: by which I mean that it absorbs strength from the texts that it hosts, the most sublime of canonical poems in Latin. For on crossing the threshold of the poem, we are soon entranced by Juvenal's parade of his poet ancestors and anxiety-figures: in particular, the central texts of Horace, *Odes* 1. 12 and Virgil, *Aeneid* 6. 756–886. You'll find detailed discussion of the *Ode* in Appendix 1, together with a text and translation (pp. 97–114). Synopsis, text and translation of the most important *exempla* from Virgil's 'roll-call of Roman heroes' are given in Appendix 2 (*Aeneid* 6. 808–86; pp. 115–22). The featured case of Virgil's Fabius Maximus, along with Livy's, and Ovid's, is explored in Appendix 3, where the discussion includes texts and translations of the chief passages (pp. 123–30). I shall also consider other important passages where Roman fame and name are on parade, but these are the key poetic matrices for Juvenal, whose writing deserves to join them on any educational syllabus. They should share a shelf in anyone's library—and indeed they claim as much.

4 IF THIS IS AN ANSWER, WHAT WAS THE QUESTION?

You'll find we don't need stuffy barons or stuffed gentry for this *Satire* to address the workings of name and fame in culture, into a third millennium. Juvenal's imagery does more than figure Roman nobility; his satire does more than disfigure it. This poet also places the charades of lineage within the wider circuitry of power-play. Maybe, even, he'll show he has the whole business of social programming figured out. To my way of thinking, this is his big moment.

So why (a cynic might sneer to a sceptic) has Juvenal's descant on the working of heredity in Roman culture attracted so little comment?[3]

- Are their nobs and nabobs really too drab for words?
- Does the worn subject of snobbery strait-jacket Satire?
- Prosopography and poetry don't mix?
- Or is it us?

Answers to these questions, and exploration of what is at stake in them, are considered through these chapters. Juvenal's famous names give Satire a perfect chance to explain its constitutive irrepressibility, in whatever polity, among whatever clan. Every hall of fame is, for the Juvenal in us, another haul of shame.[4]

So read through the *Satire*, and then take a walk through *our* post-imperial museum culture. Amuse yourself wondering where *we* stand. What do the first words of the poem add up to now?

- *Stemmata quid faciunt?* (v. 1)
- Pedigrees: what do they give rise to?

For example:

- Is a *sense of* history bunk?

However daft the answers, we'll be thinking about something important, even helping to decide where nobility and virtue are heading. If they are. Or ever were.

CHAPTER ONE

ON THE WAY IN: TEXT AND TRANSLATION OF JUVENAL, *SATIRE* 8. 1–38

1 TEXT

*Stemmata quid faciunt? quid prodest, **Pontice**, longo*
sanguine censeri, pictos ostendere uultus
*maiorum et stantis in curribus **Aemilianos***
*et **Curios** iam dimidios umerosque minorem*
* **Coruinum** et **Galbam** auriculis nasoque carentem?*   5
quis fructus generis tabula iactare capaci
*?**Fabricium**?, post haec multa contingere uirga*
fumosos equitum cum dictatore magistros,
*si coram **Lepidis** male uiuitur? effigies quo*
tot bellatorum, si luditur alea pernox,   10
*ante **Numantinos**, si dormire incipis ortu*
luciferi, quo signa duces et castra mouebant?
*cur **Allobrogicis** et magna gaudeat ara*
*natus in Herculeo **Fabius** lare, si cupidus, si*
uanus et Euganea quantumuis mollior agna,   15
si tenerum attritus Catinensi pumice lumbum
squalentis traducit auos emptorque ueneni
frangenda miseram funestat imagine gentem?

tota licet ueteres exornent undique cerae
atria, nobilitas sola est atque unica uirtus. 20
Paulus uel Cossus uel Drusus moribus esto,
hos ante effigies maiorum pone tuorum,
praecedant ipsas illi te consule uirgas.
prima mihi debes animi bona. sanctus haberi
iustitiaeque tenax factis dictisque mereris? 25
agnosco procerem: 'salue Gaetulice, seu tu
Silanus, quocumque alio de sanguine rarus
ciuis et egregius patriae contingis ouanti'—
exclamare libet populus quod clamat Osiri
inuento. quis enim generosum dixerit hunc qui 30
indignus genere et praeclaro nomine tantum
insignis? nanum cuiusdam Atlanta uocamus,
Aethiopem Cycnum, prauam extortamque puellam
Europen; canibus pigris scabieque uetusta
leuibus et siccae lambentibus ora lucernae 35
nomen erit pardus, tigris, leo, si quid adhuc est
quod fremat in terris uiolentius. ergo cauebis
et metues ne tu sic Creticus aut Camerinus. (vv. 1–38)[5]

2 TRANSLATION

Pedigrees, now, what's their game?

What's in it, **Ponticus**, to be rated high for elongated
Yonks of blue blood; to run tours round the portraits of
Family faces: there, stuck on board the chariot, **Aemilians**,
And **Curius**es, half what they were; a touch short in the shoulders,
Corvinus, and **Galba**, both ears and nose not there? 5

What's the cut, for flaunting on a jumbo family-chart
Fabricius(?); and, next, for confecting a crop of lines
To link grimy Cavalry Captains and their Commandant,
If in sight of **Lepidi** lives a bad lot?

6

What good are all the likenesses
Of warrior hosts, if it's all a game, a gamble through the night,   10
With **Numantines** looking on, if your sleep starts when dawn
Comes up, when Generals of old stirred troops and struck camp?

Why should a son find joy in **Allobrogics** and High Altar,
Born in the **Fabian** house, Hercules' shrine, if grasping, if
Inane, and soppier as you please than any *bien-né* Venetian
    lamb,   15
If rubbed down with pumice *Catinese*, all succulent tenderloin,
He puts unkempt forefathers on parade, and as The Purchaser of
    Poison
His likeness merits smashing, he casts a pall on the stricken clan?

For all that antique casts perfect the décor all around—
Whole halls full—yet Nobility is *non pareil*, inimitable, when it
    means Virtue.   20

Paulus, Cossus, Drusus. . .—become one of them, with their
    traits;
Put *those* before your family ancestor portraits;
Let *them* clear the way for the magistrate's parade of power,
    lined-up for a consul like you.

First thing you owe me: goodness of mind.

        Regarded as 'a saint,
He never gave up on Right'—are you worth that, what you do, all
    you say?   25

I spot some High-up: 'Greetings, **Gaetulicus**—or you're a
Silanus, whatever other bloodline you're from—citizen
Extraordinaire, that cut above the rest, acclaimed blessing on your
    country.'

—I want to shout loud what the folk shout for Osiris
Found.

You see, whoever's going to say someone has breeding
   who   30
No way matches the breed, and the name, fairest of fair, is the
   only way
He stands out?

Someone's dwarf, giant 'Atlas' we call him;
Their Nigerian's the original snowy 'Swann'; that no-good,
   disfigured girl is
'Miss Beau Monde'; or a pack, now, gone to sloth, through
   chronic mange
Bare of coat, dogs licking oil-lamp's face-grease dry as a bone: 35
For name they'll be 'Panther', 'Tiger', 'Lion' . . . or whatever's
   yet to come,
Roaring anywhere on earth more savagely still.

That is why you'll take care,
And fret—is this you? called '**Creticus**', or called '**Camerinus**',
   just so,
               —but called it how?
                                    Like that?   38

CHAPTER TWO

NOBLESSE OBLIGE: WHAT ARE PEDIGREES?

- *Stemmata quid faciunt?* (v. 1)

In these opening words, *Satire* 8 at once names its topic:

- The function of *The Pedigree*.

'What are pedigrees for?' raises a traditional kind of question for ancient moralistic discourse, one well-supplied with traditional answers. Juvenal's diatribe duly serves them up, more or less. So his 'question' functions, among other things, as a prompt which cues in a sermon. A sermon that feeds, inevitably, on jeeringly destructive questioning of tradition, to clear a path for what, in some hands, can issue in a higher ethics. First deplore trading on ancestral laurels, runs the recipe, then lift aspirations somewhere, anywhere, higher. In Juvenal's disquisition, though, the approach will keep swinging toward and away from saying the right things wrong; sending up the very idea of saying right things on the subject; and dropping the topic as traditionally conceived altogether, in favour of de-glamorized latter-day preoccupations—what Hadrian's second-century CE Rome had to look forward to, *instead*.

The poem is not *all* cynical derogation, I suppose. It does come out and tell the world to be a better place, where everyone tries to 'better'

9

themselves. But along the way the topic proves to be another ideal opportunity for rubbishing all manner of shibboleths and sacred cows, particularly in the realm of 'the dead who occupy the old family-tombs that line the roads into Rome', which Juvenal's first programme finally proposed to make the stamping-ground of his poetry.[6] In the Roman *atrium* (hall) stocked with *imagines* (ancestor portraits), Satire plays the same scene of surveillance under the policing gaze of the ancestors, only *inside*, at the juncture between the comings and goings that link domestic with urban-metropolitan life. Nowhere is sacred, no door closed to the satirist's proboscis, certainly not the corridors of the nobility. His reach claims this threshold conduit linking interior privacy and the public highway for the social realm of civic intercourse. So, if the question is:

- *Stemmata quid faciunt?*

a first, forthright answer might be:

- 'Pedigrees make ideal stuff for Satire.'

Perhaps this *Adelssatire* (Satire on Nobility) *likes* the ingenious digs and ingenuous teases it thinks and throws up far too much? No matter what they decide, reciters and readers have to choose quite how to slant their performance, and their audience and they must make their own guesses, and so *their own views*, plain in the process. And that is very much the point: the bite, or tweak, of Satire on its participants. Indeed we are all born players when it comes to this subject of transmitted privilege and skeleton in the cupboard, of talents passed on or gone to seed. It makes waves clear across any social panorama. So the script exposes all us Juvenals that play its theatre. We're here for the amateur stemmatics.

- Q: 'Not dusting off Debrett's *Peerage*?'
- A: 'The subject of *pur sang* implicates and unsettles *any* audience, guarantees drama.'

So far so good. Now let's look harder into pedigrees. These are kinship-structures, good to think with, even better to pretend with.

These semiotic matrices of order use patterning through generational and affinal (in-law) relationships to model and project signification into collective and competitive weighing out of a *status quo*, and to determine what will replace that. Societies stake out their contests for the various kinds and hierarchies of cultural power on the axis of capital invested in the past, plotted against the circumstantial thrust of the present. Genealogy is one cluster within a society's ideological apparatus through which pressure is brought to bear toward realizing a future in conformity with a valued representation of the past. Oligarchies have traditionally been constituted (invested with charisma, legitimated, rationalized) through a blend of 'aristocratic' discourses supplemented by recourse to an alliance of pragmatic and principled counter-arguments and directives. It is patent that no oligarchy can ever come anywhere close to *being* a thoroughbred 'aristocracy', since the past is a burden as well as a make-weight or engine-room for any regime as it seeks or consolidates legitimacy. Rather, lineage is factored into the necessary negotiation of access and entry into the ranks of an élite, to absorb the variables of changing circumstance and the differential trajectory of power-blocs. Lineage, in short, is a fungible in the representation of status within a *status quo*. Hence:

- A: 'What pedigrees do, is constitute specific arguments within the politics of homoeostasis (resistance to change).'

What *questioning* gentility (family distinction) does, on the other hand, is court destabilization of the working of hereditary systems in the operation of civic institutions, by focusing on the few who enjoy the privilege which these deliver. Especially in a public forum where the sabotaged convene to discover their handicapping. Lotteries work so long as people see themselves as big winners, at worst little losers, and no rigging. But families are where people traditionally look(ed) forward to rigging the future, motivated to give progeny (i.e. sons) a better, or no worse, start than fathers had. Heredity traditionally plays a paradigmatic role for all other bequests, the range of efforts to 'own' a portion of the future. Thus the bottom line is that 'aristocracy'

11

underpins stable transmission between generations of whatever is valued. Accordingly, our first salvo *should* be:

- A: 'What *blue blood* does, is mystify parental investment in children—"their" children.'

For each citizen, knowing the history of their state competes with the variety of closer knowledges of the panoply of family, clan, tribe groupings which every one of them must acquire. People belong, and are real, according to the distribution of *both* these sets of knowledge, and in the weave and friction of their interfacing.

So this is the next point to consider: cultural competence is built into the creation of self and others. It materializes in positioning persons, places, calendar events and commemorative occasions appropriately. It is shaped and emphasized by educational curricula and classroom instruction. It is put into operation, with various premiums and penalties, through the public institutions of social, political, religious life. It is realized more or less formally, expressively, or playfully, in the etiquettes, politesses and norms of off-duty social intercourse. And it is glamorized in all the productivity of the apparatus of wisdom, the professors and their handbooks, the experts and their lore. 'Oligarchies' slant history toward the recuperation of select individuals to the benefit of wider socio-political structures: hagiography (textual beatification) of fathers and father-figures plays a paradigmatic role in this process.

- A: 'Family trees make people privilege some aspects of their cultural repertoire above others.'

As you see, the subject of 'birth' soon gets to be a big one. The logic (the phrase *quid faciunt* suggests 'functional analysis' of *stemmata*) of the aristocratic imperative is that it sets at odds the priority of the long-established and as such no longer so deserving family, over the family of today which deserves the best future, but is down-shifted by the inferiority of late-comer posteriority. Instant promotion is at once impossible and necessary: it is wanted for self, but destroys stability for all. The principle of precedence puts down upstarts as bad precedents which newcomers are bound to regret, the moment they have, impossibly, joined the establishment.

- A: 'Genealogy sets family against family, history against history, value against value. It generates friction; and fast-breeds indignation.'

Besides, 'birth' concerns not just gentility, nor only family and inter-familial claims made for and against recognition of the value of descendants, but rather *all* competing 'axiological-deontological systems' (the nexus of thought and utterance regulated between considerations of worth and of duty) that dispute truth, power and authority, in whatever social arenas. Families may not be *devoid* of worth, but (like states) they are no more than a yardstick to calibrate greater ideals against. At some moments, to some points of view, principles that *aren't* thicker than blood must have been watered down. There simply have, at times, to be stronger motives than the accidental ties of birth. Moreover, against the pull of lives and communities along the channels of family and national aspirations and fixations, there is ranged also the need to put power into the right hands *now*, *here*, in *this* area, whether or not they are 'safely' endowed with a certified family past. That's politics.

- 'What *stemmata* do, is arouse sanctimonious moralizing.'

Or, to put it another way, Juvenal's enquiry could be out to prove he is facing his greatest challenge:

- 'Those *imagines* in the hall—they concern *everything*.'

CHAPTER THREE

ROME IN THE *NOMEN*: NAMING IN LATIN

At Rome, bids to assert dominance in the name of certain family records always struggled against, and colluded with, their other social-political concerns. Top-drawer families made themselves famous where they could, and *arrivistes* paid more than lip-service to this business by rustling up some fitting past for their *domus* (household).[7] A great deal of investment went into the prestige industry, supplying advice, creating charisma, inventing and determining tradition. In turn, the merchants of cultural expertise could use their grip on the aristocratic heritage to play for authority of their own. By Juvenal's day, the historian, the epitomator, the anthologizer, the declaimer, the preacher and the philosopher all needed to know, not just their material, but also the stock of routines. Plus the history of their crafts, and even the 'pedigree' of their trades in Roman culture.[8]

Moreover, any treatment of *nobilitas* cannot avoid plugging the Greek 'equivalent' (*eugeneia*) into Roman sockets, and along with it, the wealth of discursive positions stocked with an arsenal of truths from Greek civilization: *mian eugeneian aretên* ('Virtue is the one nobility'), for one, neither a solitary nor unique gem.[9] Romans could at most *pretend* to exorcize Hellenic doctrine from their thinking: this they did in aristocratic moments—before Republican elections, and at upper-

14

crust funerals, for example. But just as Hellenic subjects in the Empire occupied themselves in re-thinking their inheritance of slogan and argument in the alien light of Roman stratifications and sentiments, so educated Romans busily worked to interpret the cargo of wisdom along and against the force-lines of their own language, the grooves of their ritual. Thus, for instance, the Greek term *stemma* itself was so thoroughly naturalized in Latin that even an arch-nostalgist would neither flinch nor flicker at using it in documenting the atavistic traditions at the heart of Roman *mores*.[10] But mapping the *gentes* (clans) was clearly *not* a prime area where Greek thinking could parade its superior grasp of analysis. Juvenal's topic, then, could, and should, be conceived as all-engrossingly chauvinistic:

- 'Family trees? They grow *Romans*.'

Let this sum up the cultural stakes. But Juvenal's question is also (take a look) the first half of a hexameter, to start Juvenal, *Book* 3, poem 2, and is coded for the reader accordingly. Hence

- *Quid stemmata faciunt?*

asks its far from remarkable question with a modal nuance all its own. The question,
'Are stemmatics a fit subject for Roman Satire?'
can easily be a sarcastic way to ask, or rather insinuate, and make a dig:

- 'Juvenal is running out of steam, is he not?'

The subject of pedigrees could easily seem to stand a long way from the first *Book*'s flurry of vice that crammed itself straight into Juvenal's 'note-books from the concrete jungle of Rome's naked city'.[11] Has Juvenal been spending too much time in his study? Isn't he turning into one of those interminable, interminably straight, and ten-a-penny performers he presented himself as displacing when he began?[12] The alternative declaimer gone straight now that he has made it?

So it could seem. But Juvenal has from the beginning profited from the canonical status of the tradition of Roman Satire.[13] His work depends on the availability of a public able to read him in his intertextual relations with the other classic Latin satirists: with the Neronian Persius (mid-first century CE); with Persius and the Augustan Horace (late first century BCE) and the Republic's Lucilius (late second century BCE); with Horace, Horace and Lucilius; and with Lucilius. These are his 'ancestors' within the genre (the literary *genus*, breed, type, race), a network of interrelated predecessors tending toward in-breeding. Thus, any interpretation of his writing must negotiate the classicist's problematic:

• '*Stemmata.* . . How *do* generic affiliations work?'

Beyond the classic texts of Satire, Juvenal derives the drive of his irate tirades from the epical bearing he gives his writing, so that this poem's parade of evocative Roman names must find its surest and most insistent reverberations in the canon of Roman epic. This important point calls for emphasis because criticism and commentary have, for no good reason, not checked half hard enough into this dominant network of generic intertextuality.

Expect, then, desecration of the litany from Aeneas' father Anchises in Virgil, *Aeneid* 6 (756–886: see Appendix 2 for synopsis, text and translation of the highlights, pp. 115–22). And of the post-Virgilian successor-rival, the ghoulish Neronian Lucan, *Bellum Ciuile* 6 (777–99); the arch-apostle Silius, faithfully Virgilianizing in the late first century CE (*Punica* 13. 613–754: past, 853–67: future); the anti-Virgilian dogmatist Manilius, writing under Tiberius (*Astronomica* 1. 775–802); and Virgil's would-be antecedent, his impersonator's natty skit *The Gnat* (*Culex* 358–71). Comparisons between these purple passages and Juvenal's are threaded through the text and notes that follow (see especially the relevant entries in the Index of Chief Passages, pp. 167–8).

The importance of such intertextual relations for reading Juvenal shouldn't need to be argued for, anyhow, but Juvenal's opening question will press the button, just in case:

• Q: 'What, you ask, are *literary* antecedents (*stemmata*)?'

16

• A: 'They make writers derivative, but they also enable them to function. Read on.'

Next, the matter of *imagines* brings us to consider art, and the literature devoted to, and directive of, art, and the connections between artistic and literary genres. As is widely recognized, Virgil's monumental 'Roll-call of Heroes' paralleled the line-up of Roman patriots in stone set along both sides of the Forum of Augustus in the approach to the marshalling statues of the dynastic patriarch Aeneas and of his opposite number, the first founding father Romulus. This pair in turn presided, between them, over the approaches to the Temple of Mars Ultor, whose pedimental sculpture had Aeneas' mother Venus accompany Romulus' father Mars.[14] These textual and sculptural narratives depicted Rome through the historical pageant of exemplary leaders, but they also imaged, interpreted and commented on their particular qualities and achievements. The ensemble twined Rome into a double helix whose tendrils assimilated the generations of Romulus' *gens Romana* to those of Aeneas' *gens Iulia*. Beneath the gaze of their divine parents, there paraded the wider 'Roman clan' and, within it, its uniquely privileged 'Julian clan'.

The point of this procession was not 'historic' but ideological, there not to record a mnemonic, but to stimulate and direct attention, interest, cathexis. The trick was for mimesis to get into the audience and visitors, get them into the procession, and surround them with a living past. So Virgil's arch-dynast Anchises anti-boasts to his son Aeneas, in what he meant for the uplifting peroration to his account of the system to which mortal existence is bound and to his praise of the heroes of Roman history, before he noticed Marcellus, and his son prodded for more:

'excudent alii spirantia mollius aera
(credo equidem), uiuos ducent de marmore uultus. . .'. (Aen. 6. 847f.)[15]

'Others will hammer out bronze statues that draw breath more delicately,
As I believe, and from the marble beckon living faces expressive as life

17

[*sc.* but look how well I have just done precisely this]. . .'.

- 'At their best, *stemmata* inspire poets to bring art to life.'

There is a connection between poetry, *atrium*, and imperial forum. But, to be sure, Juvenal's harangue is not out to consecrate and inculcate by commemoration. Rather, he is out to desecrate and denigrate, by exploiting his audience's fluent literacy in the lore of heroism. Taking the story of Roman greatness as read, the poet will re-assemble the procession of great names—only carnivalized and carved into caricature lumps. So here in this poem, the question

- 'What do pedigrees have going for them?'

signals that Juvenal plans to come into the holiest legacy of Roman poetry: the dramatized synthesis of the chain of builders of the Roman Empire, as narrated by the Roman historians and put into epic verse: by Ennius, back at the Republic's triumph over Hannibal's Carthage; by the Augustan Virgil; and, just before Juvenal, by the Flavian poet Silius. And Juvenal plans to blow the lot, like any *nepos* (grandson/spendthrift). You have been warned:

- A: 'Pedigrees line up scalps for iconoclasts.'

Each brave Roman soldier had a place of pride in the family-stakes of his *gens*, and epic and history undertook to position his fame as another step in the Empire's eternal march to glory. Inclusion in Ennius' verse or in the Augustan Livy's prose, in the *Aeneid* or in Silius' *Punica*, like other national honours, bequeathed fame to descendants on just those terms. For posterity, the stories of greatness won would reside in these canonized texts. Thus, for all that the old Republican *gentes* survived only in texts, Hadrianic Rome could not manage to think without them, in all its conclusive posteriority.[16] They still set the benchmark for patriotism.

This inheritance of writing mimed and led the Roman élite's factory-belt of practices and ceremonies designed to enhance its standing by accumulation of ancestral glory. The culture manufactured media and products which stressed the stake of the past in the oligarchic present,

18

as a blind for the prosecution of ascendancy in the present, through the symbolic tokens of the past. Arrayed portraits and statues, inscriptions at family tombs, and (before all—before all residents and visitors) the concise family trees painted on the walls of the *atrium*, and the lines of *imagines* and rows of busts set out along the same walls, conditioned and ushered in every entrée to the current incumbent of each family destiny.

Only those who had won the honour of magistracy were supposed to appear as *imagines* in their descendants' Hall of Fame.[17] These normative representational displays of glory in the order of the *domus* broadcast fame in their own idiom. They depended on the cultural valency of the verbal system of nomenclature, which inscribed and framed Roman individuality within the orbit of the ancestors. The *paterfamilias* (head of the family, father-figure) was the chief bearer of fame, which he carried within his name (*nomen* means 'fame' as well as, as the equivalent of, 'name').

Juvenal will explain:

• 'The Peerage has ways to sanctify names.'

Traditional patterns of the Roman nobility assigned identity through the *nomen* that indicated the clan sub-group of society; and the individuating function of the *praenomen* (forename), taken from a restricted traditional range, was often supplemented by the *cognomen* (supplementary name), which might mark a personal nickname, filiation, or separation of a clan-segment from others within the *gens*.[18] Within such schemata, some top-notch individuals could stamp their own fame on their *gens*, so that future Romans would treat them as irreplaceable eponyms, overshadowing anything their descendants might ever achieve. For example, as we shall find before Juvenal 8 is done, *Marius* made sure, in effect, that there would only ever be one *Marius*; such was his domination of the gentilician 'fame'. Far more heroes, however, inhered in their *cognomina*, no matter what the deserts of those who took their names. *Sulla*, for one, made it hard for anyone who came later to own and re-colour the name/fame.[19] *Very special* citizens could grow extra titles, as in the 'triumphal' *cognomen*

19

ex uirtute (supplementary name conferred as a badge of courage) where a conqueror took on the name and fame of his conquest: e. g. Fabius *Allobrogicus* (v. 13), conqueror of the Gallic tribe of Allobroges.[20] So signal an *agnomen* (additional name) was particularly sure to follow the estate through the generations to come. But other ways to become polyonymously special were legion. In particular, it even became an advantage to proclaim adoptive status in certain circumstances, so as to retain the kudos of the family of origin, in combination with that of the acquired family. Thus the name of Scipio *Aemilianus* (v. 3) publicizes the adoption into the Cornelii Scipiones of someone born an Aemilius.[21]

In the Late Republic, Rome's proto-imperial generalissimos developed a regal style of power-packed nickname to advertise the extraordinary status which explained why they behaved in such irregular ways: Sulla *Felix* (Lucky), or Pompeius *Magnus* (The Great). Finally, with the Emperors came a new dimension in superb nomenclature, *Imperator* (General) becoming a strange forename (Emperor), the beatific *Augustus* (Well-omened) amplifying the key title *Caesar* (formerly a long-hallowed *cognomen* of the Iulii) with a Messianic aura. Our Claudius, *Imp. Ti. Claudius Caesar Augustus Germanicus* (born Ti. Claudius Drusus), could leave Rome to our Nero, his (adoptive) son *Imp. Nero Claudius Caesar Augustus Germanicus* (born L. Domitius Cn. f. Ahenobarbus); once, *Claudius Nero* had been the famous Republican name borne by a proud sub-clan (as *nomen + cognomen*).[22] Imperial courtiers joined in a fantasy 'restoration of the old ways' with zest, by reviving rows of names for fame, accumulating and distributing them in their *new* ways: a *Cn. Cornelius Cinna Magnus* could inherit 'greatness' (*Magnus*), through his mother Pompeia; a *M. Licinius Crassus Frugi* (son of a Calpurnius Piso) and a *Scribonia* could produce, through a mixture of adoptive and maternal dynastics, their sons *Cn. Pompeius Magnus, M. Licinius Crassus, Scribonianus*, and *Piso Licinianus*,[23] and (adoptive, testamentary) names like [*Q. Iulius Cordinus*] *C. Rutilius C. f. Gallicus* became unexceptional, even modest, in the imperial entourage.[24] Ever more creative fiction positioned social personhood in a stratosphere of names and titles drawing on an ever longer span of Roman history. This is the expansive field that Juvenal undertakes to examine:

> Q1. **Either** (a). . . *illustris animas nostrumque in nomen ituras*. . . ('famous souls destined to come into our name', Virg. *Aen.* 6. 758). Discuss.
>
> **Or** (b) Names present members of the élite as phases in a family history: analyse the logic, using words, not diagrams.

The way I shall approach the subject of Roman genealogy is by positing that a rhetoric of antonomasia (the provision of equivalent substitutes for a proper name) effected a strategic nexus of language with truth and power, and paradigmatically infused Roman culture with 'nobility' as the permanent currency of prestige. It is true that Juvenal's text tilts the enquiry toward literature; but this should not take us off into the realm of imagery, and away from the reality of politics. Rather:

• 'Take the lid off the cultural poetics of the Roman pedigree, and what do you see?'

CHAPTER FOUR

PEDIGREE CHUMS: THE POETICS
AND POLITICS OF ROMAN NAMES

- *Stemmata quid faciunt?* (v. 1)
  'Pedigrees, now, what's *their* game?'

starts the *Satire*. And we are almost ready to press on with our reading.

Bucked by the metre, but also (thank goodness) by the enormity of it all, poets *could* not write into their texts a large percentage of Roman nomenclature; not with the best will in the world. Besides, the range of forms of address made possible through the proliferation of the élite individual's titles presented, in literature as well as in life, an ever more refined art of formality/intimacy, distance/solidarity, encomium/vituperation in the rhetoric of appellation.[25] A full naming was not necessarily the obvious or maximal tribute to offer a grandee. Instead, the intrinsic meaningfulness of most elements in the Roman name— particularly once it was filled out by the etymological and interlingual inventiveness and audacity of scholars, antiquarians, poets and other authority-figures—provided a well-stocked world of ready-made imagery and this loosed the referential function of naming into a spree of associative verbal/conceptual play.

Since the *cognomen*, especially, had always and forever seized on particular personal characteristics or qualities ('That nose, that forehead, those feet. . .', 'How shrewd, what a good son. . .'), the stories behind nicknames made for colour and customized fame trumpeted through the name. Since the preservation and elaboration of traditional nicknames blurred into an industry of designer-labels meant to fore-or-dain descendants' prestige, especially in the form of those triumphal surnames, the bestowal and acceptance of names turned into a vital game for the imagination of both the players and their writers. They all applied what may be nicknamed 'poetic' thinking to the business of nomenclature, though names portrayed claims to fame as much out of artistic contexts as within them.

Thus the Roman epigraphic addiction made inscriptions a central medium for profiling the desired image of the agents of the World State: a name read as a complex synthesis of meanings that derived from the ordinary currency of words hijacked for names; from the associations evoked by reference through the name back to the bearer(s) who made it famous and so valuable currency in re-circulation; and (not least) from the inclusion of these word-fame-names in the canonical texts which hallowed their contents throughout the length and breadth of Latin reading-culture. Incised or penned, names micro-packaged the encyclopedia of Rome to the ends of their earth. Names trailed the stories of an *ancien regime*.

Poets could produce acute, or cute, dramatizations of the fame within the compass of the legendary name, by exploring the semantics, by exploiting their high interpretivity and its accessibility to the literate public, and (not least) by expanding the weight of their references to individuals through the manipulation of minimal, so maximally gener-alized, titles: the bare mention of (a) *Lentulus* or (a) *Brutus*, *tout court*, could not fail to activate the fame/name of a whole 'crop' of Cornelii Lentuli,[26] and hang the legends of the Iunii Bruti on some friend who sported the *Liberator*'s evocative *cognomen*.[27]

Anti-poets could take up the negative capability within this play with the proper name. The satirist historian Tacitus could drown the state funeral rites supervised by the Emperor for a loyal intimate with the mock-scrupulous note that he had always called the deceased *Quirinius* rather than *Sulpicius Quirinius*, not because it wasn't his name, but

23

'because he had nothing whatever to do with the patrician family of Sulpicii'.[28] The retention of slave-names within the titles of non-Italian enfranchisees imported a tempting cornucopia of disgust through attention to the stories and imagery in their names: when *Scipio Cornelius* proposes thanks to the *libertus* (former slave) *M. Claudius Pallas* 'for putting his *ueterrimam nobilitatem* ['most ancient nobility'] second to public interest, by allowing himself to play the Emperor's servant despite being sprung from the kings of Arcadia', we can smell sarcasm, even if we can't be sure quite whose it is, and on whom it is turned; when reference to Pallas' brother *Felix*'s name follows, 'sure he could do anything without fear of consequences because he reposed on such huge power', Romans must think: 'Shades of another Cornelius, his lordship *Sulla* Felix'.[29] Or take the debate between Claudius' *liberti* triumvirate, out to pick him a new wife as if they were the true imperial *consilium* (think-tank): this is awash in the disgrace of their bandying to-and-fro of great names and their claims: *Narcissus* was for Aelia Paetina *e familia Tuberonum* ('from the house of the Tuberones'), *Callistus* plumped for Lollia Paulina, daughter of a *consularis* (former consul), and *Pallas* rooted for Iulia Agrippina, daughter of Germanicus, with his grandson for a bonus, who 'would join together a noble stock and the descendants of the Julian and Claudian families'.[30] Again, snide Lucan can have *Brutus* enter the text in command of the Caesarian fleet out to destroy the Massilian/Phocaean navy's defence of Republican *Libertas*/Greek *Eleutheria*, without a hint that this is *D. Iunius Brutus Albinus*, not the *M. Iunius Brutus* who earlier dropped in on Lucan's Cato.[31]

Whether or not they are making a dog's breakfast of *mos maiorum* (the ancestral tradition), much of the punch of heavyweight Latin writers stems from the verbal-conceptual play of all this onomatopoetics (inventive thinking through names).

CHAPTER FIVE

IT'S NO GOOD CALLING PEOPLE NAMES: vv. 1–5

- . . . *quid prodest,* **Pontice,** *longo*
sanguine censeri, pictos ostendere uultus
maiorum et stantis in curribus **Aemilianos**
et **Curios** *iam dimidios umerosque minorem*
Coruinum *et* **Galbam** *auriculis nasoque carentem?* (vv. 1–5)

. . . What's in it, **Ponticus,** to be rated high for elongated
Yonks of blue blood; to run tours round the portraits of
Family faces: there, stuck on board the chariot, **Aemilians,**
And **Curiuses,** half what they were; a touch short in the shoulders,
Corvinus, and **Galba,** both ears and nose not there?

This first amplification of Juvenal's topic establishes that he means to
hang his thoughts on *stemmata* around the neck of an addressee-victim.
He is dubbed *Ponticus* because, as well as being a real enough name, it
is used for a series of victims in one of Juvenal's most important sources
for scurrilous defamation, the *Epigrams* written by Martial at the end
of the first century CE; but most of all because it has the feel of a
triumphal name, commemorating an ancestor's conquest of *Pontus,*
which will provide prime material for this sentence and later in the

25

poem. *Ponticus* might, however, alternatively brand its bearer the descendant of non-citizen stock from the far eastern edge of the Empire:[32] the very juxtaposition *Pontice, longo* (v. 1) can suggest as much. At once, our grasp of Roman prosopography is put to the test. And we readers are all put under the microscope.

The question put to Ponticus asks:

• *quid prodest. . . censeri?* (v. 1f.)

This catches for him the tone of a noble protesting his right to privileged consideration:[33] but Juvenal is, at once, treating 'the blood-line' as a commodified good which covers its concrete business in mystificatory stylization: *longo / sanguine* (v. 1f., 'long blood') is the poem's first verbal decoction of 'The Pedigree'. Referential synonymy may obtain between *stemmata* and *sanguis*, but the phrase is a crashing catachresis (abuse of language) from this anti-poet. 'Long blood' puts the squeeze on the core terms-and-concepts of the apparatus of 'nobility'. Triumphs were supposed to require an enemy death-toll above five thousand, the crude measure of the worth of imperatorial *uirtus*. It therefore attested a 'long trail of blood', stretching over the wastes of some outback many a long campaign's march from home, matched by the long train of the triumphal procession through Rome. To tell of such a feat calls for blood-letting through the length of some noble epic, some one-thou-sand-page History. For the satirist, blue blood is bought with real blood.

'Rating by long blood' promises prolonged demystification of the blood-line, and the last words of Juvenal's poem will return us to the title-page, by telling us to 're-wind any and every book of fame' (*ut longe repetas longeque reuoluas nomen. . .* , vv. 272–5).[34] For the first in *any* long line, if you go back far enough, can only have been one of Romulus' unspeakable founders of Rome. Moreover, going back on the *poetic* ancestry of Juvenal will show he has at once taken us on the longest trek imaginable, down to the bowels of poetic hell, there to climb up to a very High Place, Virgil's Elysian tumulus:

> . . . *unde omnis* **longo ordine** *posset*
> aduersos legere et uenientum dis*cere* **uultus**. (*Aen.* 6. 754f.)

From where he (Anchises/Aeneas) could note them all in the long
column
in front of him, and learn the faces as their owners approached.

> . . . *quid prodest, Pontice, longo*
> *sanguine censeri, pictos ostendere uultus* (Juv. 8. 1–2).[35]

Like any long-suffering *pater*, the satirist will play Anchises to Ponticus'
Aeneas. Readers (reciters and audience) of this poetry have to see these
are their roles, too:

- 'The subject of *stemmata* hands the satirist the opportunity to talk
  down to his reader.'

Taking the 'long' view through time is the stock-in-trade of the
genealogist, and now the vehicle for mockery at his expense. But taking
the long view already commits the satirist to an antiquarian world of
long-dismantled weapons in the names-race: triumphal names, for
instance, marked *Republican* fame, for (along with triumphs) they dried
up long since. Save for *royal* conquerors, the Emperors, who monop-
olized all such kudos. Tame stuff, the *Aeneid*, all it dares is 'the
inoffensive pitch of Aeneas *vs.* the brute Rutulian': so Juvenal's first
poem had dared tell us, as if he meant it.[36] Can Juvenal, the satirist, not
the epic poet, tie the far-fetched lore of a lost world to the putative
present of his target addressee, and through him the reading-lives of
his target audience?

- 'Isn't *The Pedigree* a terrific way to bind the reading of time-worn
  classics into satiric experience of the present? Is it?'[37]

The poem's second visualization of lineage is literally that, a *visuali-
zation*: *pictos ostendere uultus* (v. 2, 'to show painted visages').
Pedigrees are a show, for show. Programmed for the reader is a
museum-gallery of artistic images, promising ecphrastic (set-piece de-
scription) verbalization of greatness.[38] Can heroism be pictured? Is

27

individuality visible? Where the face does duty for the person, is there anything else on view beside looks?

We can see the phrase as gesturing towards, on the one hand, the original face-painting with Jovian vermilion endured by every *triumphator* on the long procession up to the Capitol; and, on the other hand, the secondary reproduction and reminder of this in the forms of two-dimensional medallion-portraits daubed along the *atrium* wall, or waxen masks highlighted with multicolour finish, even touched-up busts or heads, whether triumphal or of lesser (state) acclaim. What the *writer* has set himself is a mimetic tilt at parodic representation, to the life, of the inner qualities of each ancestral character, a caricature of the collective sum of icons lovingly fashioned by so many hands over the centuries.

- 'Nobility on show? A tall order, that calls for a technocrat among iconophiles (lovers of images).'

Another great poet had made a similar start: *Ouk adriantopoios eim', host' elinusonta ergazesthai agalmat' ep' autas bathmidos / hestaot'* (Pindar, *Nem.* 5. 1f., 'I'm no statue-maker, turning out images that will take a rest, stood up on the same pedestal'). Juvenal makes the same promise of animated verbal pyrotechnics. Enter: the mimetic performer.

Envisage each visage tinted with 'superior greatness': made by 'ancestors' and showing off 'ancestors', they should be 'larger-than-life-size', 'larger than ours', they must somehow contrive to be 'bigger than their own dimensions' (*maiorum*, v. 3). On their way into someone else's *domus*, Romans could read the writing beneath the images, discover the identity of each: broadly speaking, however, they should be able to put one common name to the whole line-up, as the singularity of a forefather links together the chain of family genetics. Here greatness was greater than the sum of the parts: the stemma spatially diagrammed a temporal figuration of one-for-all, all-for-one gentilician solidarity. Roman individuality was programmed here.

CHAPTER SIX

CANST THOU NOT REMEMBER QUINTIUS, FABRICIUS, CURIUS, REGULUS?: THE 'GENERALIZING PLURAL' IN LATIN[39]

Now Juvenal's pilot-sentence itemized a run of case-studies, in two contrastive pairings:

Aemilianos / *et* **Curios, Coruinum** *et* **Galbam.** (vv. 3–5)

To generalize at once, in such cases as the first pair of names, we need to attend carefully to *generalizations.* Just such lists are a key feature of Latin discourse, and they can be tricky to understand. How are we to proceed? Scholarly wisdom[40] traditionally invokes the following rule:

[i]   'The *generalizing plural* is common in lists of *exempla.*'

Application may not run smoothly:

[ii]   '. . . [O]ne is tempted to take it in this way in our passage also. . ..
       Yet *here* we have five singulars and only one plural; therefore it is
       also possible that Horace is thinking of more than one Scaurus' [i.e.
       Scauros is the solitary plural in Horace's list of Roman 'Olympians'
       in *Carm.* 1. 12. 37].

Nevertheless, try to implement the rule:

[iii] 'Most editors assume that Horace is referring to the most famous bearer of the name, M. Aemilius Scaurus. . ... However, another Scaurus has claims to be considered:. . . this was M. Aurelius Scaurus.'

You may find yourselves stuck:

[iv] 'It is not altogether easy to choose between these two Scauri: the former is the more characteristic hero of *exempla*, the latter is much better suited to our context.'

But *don't* blame your author:

[v] 'It is possible, of course, that Horace has confused the two; yet they were comparatively recent figures.'

Rather, conclude that the rule doesn't apply *here*:

[vi] 'It seems more likely that he is alluding vaguely to both at once.'

And finally, in a cryptic parting-shot, problematize the rule as such:

[vii] 'The choice between a real and a rhetorical plural may be rather an artificial one.'

Early in this analysis (i.e. in the middle of what I have called [ii] above), the rule of the 'rule' appealed to parallels:
'The alternation of singular and plural is not unusual; cf. . . . Juv. 8. 3ff. . . .'.

Indeed reading Juvenal 8 must, inevitably, feature the reciprocal directive to 'cf. . ... *Odes* 1. 12. . ..'. So we really have no choice in the matter. To get further with what Juvenal is up to with his catalogue of names, we really must examine the 'generalizing plural' further in the Horatian instance.

Detailed analysis will be reserved for Appendix 1, after the main body of the text, so as not to distract us from following Juvenal's poem; but as will be shown there, the *Ode*, Virgil's roll-call in *Aeneid* 6, and Juvenal's *Satire* must be grasped together in any approach to the problem of the generalizing plural in Latin poetry. This is more interesting, anyway counts for more, than you might suppose.

To anticipate (or recapitulate), the reading presented in the Appendix will show that, and why, invocation of this rule can *never* be adequate to *any* catalogue or citation of *exempla* in *any* text. The rule only forecloses on the reading of specifics, for writings are always themselves exemplary; their textuality moves between the web of inter-implicated discourse and their own unique and solitary difference.[41] Thus, Juvenal's names are contextualized within the discourse of *stemmata*, and Horace's names are sited within the deployment of an encomiastic structure. The signification of their texts simply cannot be generalized outside those scenarios.

Even if we could agree to find in Horace's *Scauros* a 'generalizing plural', and if we moved conclusively to *choose* our single referent, the hymn's project would still require us to ponder this reminder that in other contexts lists of such plurals proliferate, whereas in the case of this *Ode*, such listing is 'quoted' as an insertion in a catalogue of (apparent) singularities. By the same token, even if we found in *Scauros* a number of particular individuals, and tracked down their stories, associations, and positionality, the hymn's project would still mean that we would do well to think out the generalizing force of *exempla* and exemplarity, whether formally marked by pluralizing locutions or not, in that quintessentially Roman preoccupation, the generation of normative paradigms of order out of the legendary force of distinguished forebears.[42] The poem is not simply reaching for unitary autarky (self-sufficiency); nor is it only a member of a family, or *genus*, of poems. Rather, it *imagines* the play between such drives.

The Horatian commentators' note 'Cf. Juv. 8. 3ff.' must function, ultimately, as a compendious imperative to relate (to) the specifics of another, very particular, poetic *atrium* lined with verbal fame-name-echo-facsimile imagery. Juvenal's *exempla* project into a poetic, epic/satiric, re-view of exemplarity which maintains high modality (insistent marking of the voice and mind producing the utterance). Performer-interpreters must work the *nomina* hard for their contribution toward Juvenal's investigation of Roman stemmatics.

31

The context for Juvenal's catalogue of heroes is his (eighth) investigation of the discourse of Roman *mores*—only this time Juvenal makes onomastic, dynastic, sarcastic, iconoclastic mayhem by playing with the proprieties of Rome's proper names.

- '*Stemmata* are a factor in the generation of classical fame, so, in satirical hands, of notoriety and blame.'

CHAPTER SEVEN

WHY THE LITTLE BOY WAS GLAD THAT EVERYONE CALLED HIM CYRIL: v. 3[43]

. . . stantis in curribus Aemilianos (v. 3)

. . . stuck on board the chariot, **Aemilians**

The twin plurals *Aemilianos / et Curios* (vv. 3f.) might be Juvenal turning to the cliché imprecisions of some Silver Latin rhetorical vacuity. These plurals may be Juvenal perpetrating, or mocking, lazy triteness. But they also point directly to the tie-in between singular exceptionality and plural solidarity which is the driving ambition of aristocratic argumentation. The bearer of the name *Ponticus* is, in principle, just one 'still' in the full-length feature-film of the *Pontici*, a would-be extra in a crowd of doubles following their Hamlet's lead.

This is why the poem goes on to repeat, reinforce and ramify this opening numbers game of plurals and singulars: with *?Fabricium?*, *equitum cum dictatore magistros, Lepidis* (vv. 7–9), *tot. . . Numantinos, Allobrogicis, Fabius* (vv. 11–4), and, later, the linguistic sports *procerem* and *Quiritem* (v. 26, v. 47: words which virtually never appear in the singular). *Drusus*, and soon *Drusorum* (vv. 21, 40), keep eyes trained on the problematic emblazoned in *nobilitas s o l a. . . atque u n i c a* (v. 20, 'the one and only nobility').

The first of our toffs, the *Aemiliani* (v. 3), may or may not have more than one face, or body. The centrality of *the* Aemilianus in the lore of the Republic picks him automatically for paradigm.[44] *P. Cornelius Scipio Aemilianus Africanus* will turn up again, implicitly or explicitly, in **Numantinos** (v. 11). If, however, we are half-ways Romanized, we know he had a brother, equally the natural son of L. Aemilius Paullus Macedonicus: *Q. Fabius Aemilianus Maximus.* Now if our poet's graphics show the brothers 'statuesque aboard *curribus*', we have to choose whether to see one 'chariot' or a 'chariot' apiece, since *currus* plural may spell a singular chariot (v. 3). Now at a real triumph, there was only one *triumphator* aboard; Fabius Aemilianus, however, did not boast a triumph. He rode with Scipio behind their natural father Paullus at *his* triumph, but never 'stood on a chariot' of his own. Only because gentry propped all their magistrates' *imagines* on chariots, whether triumphal or not, would Fabius tower aloft, when they were driven out for a funeral, worn by actors—minus his brother's *ornamenta* (regalia).[45]

The story encapsulated in the *Aemilian* name, nevertheless, is part of a legendary family's story: these first aristocrats of our poem were both adopted into their famous *gentes*, becoming respectively the 'great-nephew' of Fabius Maximus Cunctator and the 'grandson' of Scipio Africanus, the heroes of the Hannibalic War. . . which (as we noticed) climaxed Ennius' celebration of Roman history, made up Livy's well-thumbed third decade, and was dusted off for Silius' titanic marathon. To call either of them *Aemilianus* could be to distinguish them from other Scipiones and Fabii in their adoptive pedigrees, and since Scipio earned his 'grandfather''s title *Africanus* in his own right by destroying the Carthage the first *Africanus* had defeated, *Aemilianus* is a useful diagnostic between the pair of *Africani*.

But *Aemilianus* trumpets the much-advertised integration of Paullus' family with their kin the Scipiones, and his son's embrace and embellishment of *both* heritages. His brotherly solidarity with Fabius lasted to the graveside, where the childless Scipio was sent off by Fabius' son, the *Q. Fabius Allobrogicus* on show in **Allobrogicis** (v. 13). *Allobrogicus* did celebrate his own triumph, and handed down his triumphal *agnomen*.

34

Thus, the first portrait(s) in Juvenal's gallery *could* once have decorated the HQ of the Cornelii Scipiones, the Fabii, and/or the Aemilii Paulli, a three-in-one squad of select patrician *gentes maiores*.[46] Fraternal generosity could put Fabius Aemilianus in a painted or carved chariot with Scipio; or the record of his father's natural progenitor could be preserved in the memory of his successful son.

This 'first family''s second-century fortunes were enshrined in their dependant Polybius' *Histories*; in the didaskalia (first production notices) for Terence's first staging of his play *Adelphoe*; and in the dramatized settings of Ciceronian dialogues. They were further celebrated in Plutarch's *Lives*. At the heart of the story is Paullus' ejection of the brothers' mother, his re-marriage and a fresh pair of sons. The older boys were successfully placed, in the two most famous clans of Rome, and yet served as staff-officers in their father's victorious overthrow of Macedon, while continuing to support their mother. But, a week each side of Paullus' triumph, the younger boys both died on him. He was buried, not by *Aemilii*, but by the elder sons he had moved out/elevated. To see, or say, *Aemilianus (or Aemiliani)* is to scroll up this whole bundle of crossed lines and poetic irony. Our very first look at the nobility leaves us looking at anything but a single solitary long blood-line.

The very first thing to know about aristocracy, it seems, is that it has always faked and fudged its way forward: Scipio *Aemilianus*, we know, preferred to hang on to his loveless wife, stayed childless, and died without adopting an heir of his own. Not only could there be no stemma for *Aemiliani* as such, he did all he could to permit no lineage through himself.[47] So Juvenal chooses to show off first a famous dead end of a name on a chart. With *Aemilianus* comes a mandate to re-think any differences we presume between nostalgia's fiction of a hey-day of true descent, long gone, and the chimerical façades that latter-day con-artists have dreamed up to hide their late-coming.

Horatian (Augustan) humility spares us all triumphal names in *Odes* 1. 12; Virgil's roll-call slides from one flurry of heroes, with the pair of **Torquatus** and **Camillus** bringing back their spoils, into the apostrophe which spares him the pain of naming the Caesar-and-Pompey mutual deathwish, and then bridges to resume the flurry by riddling with the withheld triumphal *agnomina* of the unnamed [L. Mummius] *Achaicus* (*caesis insignis Achiuis, Aen.* 6. 837, 'distinguished for slaughter of Greeks') and [L. Aemilius Paulus] *Macedonicus* (destroyer of the last of the royal *genus* boasting *Aeacid* descent, v. 839). Juvenal hits at once on *Aemilianos*, knowing that this raises the conundrum of inter-familial 'adoptive nobility', and at the same time queers the force of the triumphal title *Africanus*, as the text imposes on us dubitation between reference to both *Africani, sub voce 'Aemiliani'*.

Yet at the same time, the plural befits the Scipiones, whose boast was that, with or without the Aemilii and Fabii, the Punic Wars were their family business from first to last, with L. Scipio a *triumphator* and admiral of the First War; his sons Cn. Caluus (*cos.* [= consul] 220) and P. Scipio in 218 respectively in command on the Spanish front, and in command as consul at the Ticinus, then overruled at the Trebia; from 217 they directed the Spanish front, until their defeat and deaths in 211. P. Scipio's son is said to have saved his father's life at the Ticinus; he was sent to save the Spanish front in 210, storming New Carthage, then invaded Africa for revenge at Zama over (old) Carthage (205–202). In 190, while Cn. Scipio's son P. Scipio Nasica conquered the Boii, *Africanus* was helping his brother L. Scipio become *Asiaticus* by crushing Antiochus the Great's Syria in Asia Minor. Two generations later, the *Aemiliani* brothers worked together famously: Scipio sacked Carthage (147–146), Fabius took charge of Spain (145–4); with Fabius for legate, Scipio sacked Numantia in Spain (134–133). *Scipionic* fame stood for the family solidarity attested in Juvenal's plural *Aemilianos*.[48]

• 'What fame can do to name, what names can do to lineage!'

CHAPTER EIGHT

CURIOUSER AND CURIOSER: v. 4

Next, we Juvenals face-paint (the) *Curios*:

et *Curios*. . . (v. 4)

Curiuses. . .

This name spells the primeval fame of *M'. Curius Dentatus* ('Born with Teeth'), bane of Pyrrhus, four times consul and double *triumphator*, once over Sabines and Samnites, once over Pyrrhus.

The book of fame is therefore re-wound from the mid-second-century 'Scipionic circle' lionized by the Late Republic, back to the pre-Punic struggle for supremacy within Italy, before triumphal names had entered the fray. The first of these arrived with the acclamation of Hannibal's conqueror Scipio as *Africanus* to seal Livy's story: 'on his example, thenceforth, people who no way matched his victory made the inscriptions attached to their *imagines* stand out famously and made their households' *cognomina* shine bright' (*A. U. C.* 30. 45. 7: *fecerunt* here is the last word of the decade devoted to the Hannibalic, or rather, finally, Scipionic, War). The same moment would seal Silius' epic to end epic, where the hero Scipio, *deuictae referens primus cognomina terrae* ('the first to bring home a *cognomen* from the territory he had conquered'), finds etymological fulfilment in triumphal closure, *securus sceptri* ('losing no sleep over a royal sceptre', *Pun.* 17. 627f. : *hic finis bello*, v. 619, 'this was the end to the war').[49]

Ennius' praises of plain-man plebeian Curius, *quem nemo ferro potuit superare nec auro* (*ap.* Cic. *De Rep.* 3. 6, 'No one could master him, with steel or gold'), launched him, past oblivion in the *Aeneid*, to join the sad faces in Lucan's Elysium, (*Decios. . . Camillum*) / *et Curios*, which Juvenal is here quoting (*Bell. Ciu.* 6. 785–7).

Besides his niche in the curious collection of *Culex*' Valhalla (v. 366, *Hic Curius. . .*), 'Mr Senator' Curius (cf. *curia*, 'senate-house') also gets into Silius' underworld courtesy of Lucan, with Ennian gilding: *nunc superos aequantem laude Camillum, / nunc auro Curium non umquam. . . amicum* (*Pun.* 13. 722f., 'now Camillus, a match for the gods in heaven in renown, now Curius, never [*sc.* nowhere in the classical canon] a friend to gold').[50]

Neither love nor money will stop our tracing any **Curios** to the unique and sole (plebeian, double *triumphator*) **Dentatus**,[51] so there is plenty to chew on in his pairing with (the) **Aemilianos**.

As we do so, it is worth pondering for a moment the plight of those Alban patriots, the *Curiatii* clan, who first overcame their hardy triple foes the Horatii brothers, only then to struggle through the rest of time for purely prosaic fame, stumped by the iron law of metre (the pattern: $-\cup-\cup$ . . ., will not fit into most metrical schemes): one or two poets daringly cured the repression by re-naming the family **Curios**, for short.[52] As Ovid twits his poor *Tuticanus* ($-\cup-\cup$), it can cost you more *pudor* (shame) than the fame you get, if your poet starts fiddling with your pronunciation (*Ex Pont.* 4. 12: neither shame nor fame anywhere near as great as the laughter that Ovid's dwelling on your problem will safely provoke in the reader. At Tuticanus' expense). Recall that the phil-Hellenizing Cornelii Scipiones themselves required poetic assistance if they were to receive their measure of praise: a (post-) Ovidian dactylic *Scipio* could fly through epic, one at a time, ever the nominative monarch of his sentences, but otherwise the clannish pride of their clubbability had to resort to the multicultural Ennius' gift of their alien *alias*: the mock-Graecism *Scipiadae*.[53]

CHAPTER NINE

FALLEN IDOLS: vv. 4–5

... *Coruinum et Galbam...* (vv. 4–5)
... **Corvinus,** and **Galba...**

Juvenal's scopic (visually keyed) massaging of his imaginary line of ancestral portraits itself 'assesses' these concrete symbols for worth (*censeri*, v. 2). *Maiores* must be shown 'outsize', so he raises Scipiones/Africani/*Aemiliani Maior* and *Minor* 'high on chariots', a plastic marvel of dynamic energy caught in static art (*stantis in curribus*, v. 3, cf. *statua*, 'statue', *curro*, 'move at speed').[54] Moving by ear (*curribus* → *Curios* → *Coruinum* → *carentem* → *coram*, vv. 3–9), Satire at once dashes its barons off their pedestals: chopping the pluralized *Curios* 'in half' (*di|midios*), Juvenal plays the iconoclast (image-smasher).

Long-in-the-tooth old Dentatus' fame told how he decimated his own troops to 'win' Pyrrhic victories: centuries later, he is but half the hero: but, we wonder, *which* half? This used to be a whole-figure likeness, the more hallowed because fallen apart with age? Or the more obviously a parable of false investment of pride in mere representation? Is this a joke misreading of what was always a half-*scale*, or half-*length*,[55] portrait, however antique or otherwise: showing, as *Aemilianos* showed a cack-handed selection of 'adoptive nobility', how moralists manufacture their pieties and persiflage out of their own hot, thin, air?

The same punning condensation of sermon, ecphrasis and folly redoubles in twin, chiastic 'stills' which set **Coruinus** and **Galba** nose-to-(missing) nose; dead ringers for each other: *umero<s?>* *que minorem* / **Coruinum-et-Galbam** *auriculisque nasoque carentem* / (vv. 4f.). The maimed *maiores* lose more bits of body, shrinking 'smaller' (*minorem*), and losing most of those 'little' projections (*auriculis*, 'earlets') that make *uultus uultus*.[56]

But who is **Coruinus**? Which Corvinus? Any Corvinus? *The* Corvinus? The name preserves its story: sons of M. Valerius *Coruus* (*coss.* VI, *triumphator* IV), who was helped in his brave monomachy against the Gallic champion by a raven (*coruus*) alighting on his helmet, then flapping in the giant's face, preserved this proto-triumphal name from the Early Republic through the centuries,[57] to be realized in stone on the helmet of Corvus' statue in the Forum Augustum line-up,[58] and to revive in the Julio-Claudian court through the dynasty of M. Valerius Messalla Corvinus, the admiral, orator and patron (Actian *cos.* 31, *triumphator* 27), his eponymous son (*Messallinus*), grandson and great-grandson (*cos.* 3; *cos.* 20CE; *cos.* 58CE).[59]

The 'Raven Hero' has 'lost a <bit in the> shoulder<s>' because it makes the cap fit: a *coruus* was also a 'battering-ram'.[60] But, as well, ravens, of course, have no 'shoulders', which set humans apart, not just from birds, but from all other beasts.[61]

Again Juvenal sees what he means to see: talking up a perfectly ordinary bust into a 'symbol [of] the decline of the noble republican ideals and traditions',[62] indeed; or pecking his own heirloom to pieces; or vandalizing the human icon to mock the vanity of its pretensions to incarnate the dead and gone; or making fun of his own efforts to write life into craven images. Did the artist plan his Coruus to be another compact Roman David beside the rippling biceps of his Goliath?

If the singular **Coruinus** has for referent every self-proclaimed descendant bearer of the name in their patrician Valerian *domus*, in our first 'properly' constituted stemma threading down the centuries, their partner is the equally representative patrician and proudly continuous singular **Galba**[63]—or, rather, their partners *are* the **Galbae**.

Our *titulus* could specify P. Sulpicius Galba Maximus (*coss.* [=

consuls] 211, 200), who took the fight to Hannibal's ally, Philip of Macedon; either of the Ser. Sulpicii Galbae (*cos.* 144; *cos.* 108); or either of the C. Sulpicii Galbae (*cos.* 5; *cos.* 22CE, his brother *cos.* 33CE).[64] But despite the run of names from ancient history, Juvenal makes sure that we are most likely to think of the shortest-lived Emperor of Rome to date, Ser. Sulpicius Galba (cf. v. 222), who boasted in his *atrium* a stemma unbroken 'since Jove mated with Pasiphae':[65] his fifteen minutes of fame ended with his slaughter and mutilation in the very middle of the Roman forum.

Grisly, but Juvenal's *imago* may show us a battered relic saved through a millennium, a carelessly mistreated carve-up of a more recent Galba, a head now so battered that it has lost all face, and could be any Galba you please (even none?). Or this may be any of the Emperor's images defaced and defamed by his equally ephemeral flash-in-the-pan murderers. In the last case, scorn those who hack at artworks as if it hurt the portrayed; and enjoy the sick joke that the featureless old lump of marble has come to look exactly the way the Emperor finally did in 69 CE, when his statues were smashed, and the lopped and chopped political football which once had been a head was fetched on a pole for the reward.[66] This is how an artist would 'best' remember him: the superannuated Emperor with the 'hooked nose'[67] and super-antique ancestry, proudest to be *pronepos* (great-great-grandson) of the 'senatorial' orator Q. Lutatius Catulus Capitolinus, who had the brainwave of trusting his 'dynasty' to adoption of the best prospect in Rome, in the shape of the equally short-lived Calpurnius Piso, the four-day Caesar.

Variously caustic reflections on the vanity of genealogical pride have poured through this first quartet of *nomina*, as the 'grammar' of nobility declined from the sublime Scipios to the hideously dehumanized hulk of **Galba**. We see. . . we see all we see, including the cruel jeer that this last aristocrat, misplaced to the heights of the throne, could neither scent nor hear, nor heed, the lesson his fate can teach *us*.

• 'What a fine mess Satire has made of its gentlefolk!'

41

CHAPTER TEN

THE FAME OF THE NAME: vv. 6–9

- *quis fructus generis tabula iactare capaci*
  ?Fabricium?, post haec multa contingere uirga
  fumosos equitum cum dictatore magistros,
  *si coram **Lepidis** male uiuitur?* (vv. 6–9)

  What's the cut, for flaunting on a jumbo family-chart
  Fabricius[?] ;and, next, for confecting a crop of lines
  To link grimy Cavalry Captains and their Commandant,
  If in sight of **Lepidi** lives a bad lot?

Juvenal's second variation on the imagery of the Roman *stemma* seems
to offer one singular name to start v. 7; a collective singular, *multa. . .
uirga*; followed by the plural *equitum. . . magistros* cantering round one
sole *dictator*; and the (generalizing?) plural *Lepidi* (vv. 8–9).

   The MSS intolerably repeat the / *Coruin(us)* of v. 5; editors delete
vv. 6–8, or emend. As often in Juvenal (and Satire in general), readers
can find a passage suspected of interpolation so good that deletion of
it on the mere grounds that the 'author' didn't write it becomes
appositely (satirically) discomfiting. Anyhow, I'm going to prefer the
Renaissance conjecture last favoured by Owen's old *Oxford Text*,
because I find / *Fabricium, post haec. . .* 'slightly more canny' than other

42

suggestions.[68] Because suspicion of an item in a text tends to distract from reception of its structure and flow, this is the place to step back for a moment and size up the composition of the proem we are studying at such close quarters.

What then is Juvenal engaged in putting together? What the rhetorical ensemble of Juvenal's opening salvo does, at any rate, is jump off four times from his topic-question in v. 1. Three times in a row, he then re-presents the imaginary *atrium* scene he constructs in vv. 1–5: in vv. 6–9; then vv. 9–12; and vv. 13–18. His own sententious conclusion from this ladder of visualized arguments will follow at vv. 19–20. First,

- 'What good is it to have an expansive genealogy?',

he keeps repeating, turning pointedly on his addressee,

- '— if someone like you. . .'.

Until finally he will intone the lesson:

- 'The moral of this is. . . '.

Analysis will show that the structuring of the whole passage (in six phases) is both exact and true:

[i] Questions/answer:
   quid? → *quid prodest?* → *quis fructus?* → *quo?* → *cur?* → *est.*

[ii] Trappings of pedigree:
   stemmata → *sanguine, . . . pictos. . . uultus* → *tabula. . . uirga*
   /. . . fumosos. . . magistros / → *effigies* → *Allobrogicis et magna.*
   . . ara. . . auos. . . imagine gentem → *ueteres. . . cerae / atria.*

[iii] Worth:
   faciunt → *censeri. . . ostendere* → *iactare. . . contingere* →
   [ellipsis with *quo*] → *gaudeat* → *licet. . . exornent.*

[iv] Parade before assessors:
   [ ] → *ostendere* → *iactare. . . coram* → *ante* → *traducit. . .*
   funestat → *exornent*

[v] Idealized anxiety-figures:
   [ ] → *Aemilianos / et Curios. . . Coruinum et Galbam* →

Fabricium. . . Lepidis → *Numantinos* → *Allobrogicis. . . Fabius
. . . auos. . . gentem* → *nobilitas. . . uirtus.*
[vi] Vast importance of topic:
[*stemmata*] → *longo* / → *capaci* / → *multa* → *tot* → *tota. . . sola
atque unica.*
[vii] Scornful address:
[ ] → *Pontice* → *si. . . male uiuitur* → *si luditur. . . si dormire
incipis* → *si cupidus, si* / *uanus. . . si. . . attritus. . . traducit. . .
funestat* → [ ].

What Juvenal has achieved by his quintuple cumulation of 'the same'
question, is an initial concentration of noble trappings, which he then
keeps on the boil by further reminders in each limb; then progress
toward ever more insistent expostulation with the target-addressee he
supplies, with 'if' upon 'if' (*si, si. . . si, si. . . si. . . si*); before he proclaims
his sweeping response to the opening question's generalized, or undi-
rected, form.

When we do reach vv. 19–20, we'll feel and realize that this caps
what has been a withering tirade. A heap of big names has dwarfed
pusillanimous degenerates, who fail to live up to them. The denuncia-
tion piles itself up mightily for all it is worth.

There's more to this than the immediate objective of landing the first
blow. The features we encounter in this opening passage (vv. 1–18) are
impressed upon us so that they may frame the whole of its poem. They
present: the moralized Hall of Fame; aggressive protreptic aimed at a
hopeful, would-be, should-be, no-hoper candidate for admission; a
whole commonwealth, aeons, libraries, canons, curricula of cultural
capital, all set to mock the ephebe (maturing youth) come late to the
run-down entropy of post-classical mentors. Too late to stand an
earthly chance; late enough to play dark sarcasm's figure of fun, as the
exemplum tradition did not blush to advertise, under the rubric *De
Seueritate Patrum in Liberos* ('On the cruelty of fathers to children').
To get the flavour of this severe pedagogy, we need a sample: here,
from the stern handbook of Roman anecdotes compiled in the early
Roman Empire by Valerius Maximus, you can learn in a trice of Silanus,

condemned by father Torquatus for corruption in provincial govern-
ment. He waited till dark, then hanged himself; Torquatus gave the
funeral a miss and instead made himself available for clients to consult.
Why?

*uidebat enim se in eo atrio consedisse in quo imperiosi illius Torquati
seueritate conspicua imago posita erat, prudentissimoque uiro suc-
currebat effigies maiorum cum titulis suis idcirco in prima parte
aedium poni solere, ut eorum uirtutes posteri non solum legerent, sed
etiam imitarentur* (Val. Max. 5. 8. 3)[69]

He saw he was settled in the hall in which stood the grim *imago* of the
famous disciplinarian Torquatus, you couldn't miss it. The thought
came to the wise hero that likenesses of ancestors, together with their
titles, were customarily put in the very front of the house, so that
descendants would not just read of their virtues, but imitate them too.

In the spirit of such compulsion on Roman fathers and sons to
intimidate and imitate, we now turn to Juvenal's next monster from
ancient history. Our Venetian MSS's *Fabricium* (v. 7) would give us
the (plebeian, double *triumphator*) Pyrrhic victor C. Fabricius Luscinus
whom Anchises could not leave in silence, sandwiched between his
brace of *Scipiadas*, and Regulus' furrows, just before the *Fabii* appear
(*Aen.* 6. 843–4; 845ff.). He regularly teams with Curius, *Fabricius
Curiusque pares* (Manil. *Astronom.* 1. 787).[70] Horace's *Ode* 1. 12 had
him close the stanza opened by Regulus, while the next stanza paired
him with Curius (. . . *Fabriciumque.* // *hunc et.* . . *Curium*, vv. 40f.).[71]
Lyric plays with the fabric of this name for fame; epic does the same:
paruoque potentem / *Fabricium* ('F., masterful with but little', *Aen.* 6.
843) names the hand-to-mouth make-do-with-what-you-have brico-
lage of a 'handyman' from Early Rome (*faber*).[72]

Juvenal's image-store also furnishes a customized *stemma* for *Fab-
ricius*: the *Satire*'s *imago* for him is word-pictured in the infinite
possibilities of *generis capaci. . . tabula*. Chuck him a 'generous plank
of wood', and he could make you the cynosure of his *gens*—the 'broad

span' of the *pons Fabricius* ('Fabricius bridge') over the Tiber. Like Curius, he has no real challengers for the fame of his gentilician name.[73]

However we like this conjectural **Fabricius**, this particular twist of the rhetorical kaleidoscope (vv. 6–9) resounds in an amplified echo. Instead of those meanly damaged goods glimpsed in vv. 4–5, a rhetorical cornucopia now pours (down the drain) generous 'abundance' (*fructus*):

> . . . tab*ula iactare capaci* / *Fabricium*
> *multa contingere uirga* / *fumosos equitum cum dictatore magistros*/.[74]

Here the *stemma* is pictured as the 'prolific criss-cross of lines' drawn over the picture-plane of the 'capacious panel'. At the same time as there are 'many' lines, there is only one single 'manifold' line, unique in its singular plurality: it all links up, or they all link up, together. Yet this maxi-umbilical that ties the 'scion' (*uirga*) into the network of kin puts him 'full many a long link' (*uirga*) way down the family-'line', far away from the grand old Republican heroes of the clan (*contingo*, 'relate in a certain degree, or *gradus*').

These particular anxiety-figures image the *atrium* afresh: 'smoky' *imagines* because venerable, because ante-diluvian, because their soot marks out the 'blackened' *atrium* for the family trophy-room (*ater*, 'black').[75] But these *maiores* are now word-painted as *magis-tros*. Since 'to keep touching someone with a *uirga*' is also 'to give a spanking with a cane' (cf. 7. 210), it spells sacrilegious presumption, an offshoot set 'to thrash his teachers'. *Cum dictatore*, 'along with the one giving the class *dictation*' (a terrible pun).

Moreover, since these are *equitum. . . magistros*, Ponticus is made 'to overwork the whip' on a pack of 'riders', not their chargers (*uirga*, rider's 'switch', e. g. Juv. *Sat.* 3. 317). 'No good' (*quis fructus. . .?*) will come of daring 'to give one-or-more dictator's lieutenant(s) a taste of their own summary medicine, along with their master'. For when the *equitum magister* did the Republican *dictator*'s 'bidding', this had typically meant a scourging with the rods of the lictors' *fasces*, for a *dictator*'s crisis-management precisely overrode civic rights. Nobody ever gave a Roman dictator a thrashing! Now that our target-victim has been puffed up with such sovereign and absolute plenipotentiary power: allowed to 'bandy about' the patriarch censor Fabricius, and 'to give the highest powers in the land a pasting', he must face up to his own performance: *coram Lepidis male uiuitur* (v. 9, 'in sight of **Lepidi** lives a bad lot').

The Republic had abjured dictators, along with their flying-squad hit-men the *equitum magistri*, since the end of the Hannibalic War. But Juvenal brings on the **Lepidi** to glare down[76] on the whipper-snapper 'Ponticus' as if they were still alive, not just veristic mimesis, because the most famous of the name, M. Aemilius Lepidus (*coss*. 46, 42, *triumphator II, pontifex maximus* and *IIIuir*), had been the pseudo-*dictator* Julius Caesar's *equitum magister*, in that abortive dry run of the Principate (46–44, after Antony in 47).

Of course, other **Lepidi** are there for us to ponder, in this generalizing (?) plural: the M. Aemilii Lepidi (*cos*. 285: the first known *Lepidus*; *coss*. 232, 220; *cos*. 216; *coss*. 187, 175; *cos*. 158; *cos*. 137; *cos*. 126; *cos*. 78); or their poor Julio-Claudian namesakes the Augustan *capax imperii* (coulda-been-Emperor) M. Lepidus Paullus (*cos*. 6 CE), and the son of L. Aemilius Lepidus Paullus and Julia Agrippina, so grandson of Scribonia, who fatally married Drusilla, only to be executed by Gaius in 39CE, after he had come as close as can be, in that *ménage à trois*, to first-in-line for the throne.[77] For all this, though, the Aemilii Lepidi found no niche in the *poets'* traditional roll-calls of heroes.[78]

For the poet Juvenal, however, **Lepidi** is another verbal icon: *lepidi* ('charmers') are *bons viveurs*, and so (by the 'catantiphrastic' logic by which a giant is nicknamed Little John) **Lepidi** are the right people to condemn wrong-'uns, wherever 'bad living' goes on (*male uiuitur*).[79]

CHAPTER ELEVEN

THAT FOR A GAME OF SOLDIERS: vv. 9–12

- *effigies quo*
tot bellatorum, si luditur alea pernox,
ante **Numantinos,** *si dormire incipis ortu*
luciferi, quo signa duces et castra mouebant? (vv. 9–12)

... What good are all the likenesses
Of warrior hosts, if it's all a game, a gamble through the night,
With **Numantines** looking on, if your sleep starts when dawn
Comes up, when Generals of old stirred troops and struck camp?

The last scene, of rakish 'bad living' under Cromwell eyes, set the stage
for this next one (*male uiuitur* → *luditur alea*). The *atrium*-images
appear this time as 'a host of warrior-statues' (*effigies. . . / tot bella-
torum*).

Looking *down* on 'Ponticus' are both 'the population of Numantia'
and 'their Roman conqueror(s)' (*ante* **Numantinos**), who once ringed
their fortress round, so successfully that the triumphal name *Numan-
tinus* marked the event for ever (Ov. *Fast.* 1. 596). The battlefront scene
is re-presented in the foyer cast-collection: picture it.

But the degenerate is not turning back the pages of history, but rather turning his own time back-to-front, 'staying up all *night* playing dice and dropping off to sleep at first *light*' (*per-nox* / ↔ / *luci-feri*). 'You', lunatic *Ponticus*, are the 'rising star' (*ortu*), and you manage to be up 'before the early bird Napoleons' (*ante Numantinos*). But only, you worm, because still gambling, into the dawn. . .

Yet this player's punishing schedule, Juvenal sees it, drives him as hard as any pocket-general: for him, the ancestral *imagines* are so many *bellatores*, the 'soldiers' he 'moves' round the board in his all-night session of *latrunculi* ('bandits': a game like draughts).

In his fashion, he does manoeuvre *ante Numantinos* ('before the beleaguered inhabitants of besieged Numantia'), if they may be the enemy 'pieces' he must outwit (Ov. *Ars* 3. 359–63 has *bellator. . . hostis. . . mouendus* in his board-game). And at the same time, just think, he takes up the tragic historian's presentation of real war as *ludum Fortunae. . ., periculosae plenum opus aleae* (Horace's vignette for Pollio's *Histories*, *Odes* 2. 1. 3, 6: 'the lottery of Lady Luck; a business full of the perils of a throw of the dice'). In war, 'the generals would get the standards on the road, and break camp at the crack of dawn' (v. 12).

For *this* 'Caesar', the die is cast every night: mobile Rome, the army striking camp, is for him just 'shifting statues' round the *atrium* HQ. In the poetics of satiric scorn, it is 'shifting *signs*'. A tin-soldier play of metaphor (*signa. . . mouebant*: the art in artillery?).

This has been a belittling infantilization of the addressee, a ticking off for being so juvenile. The *Satire* has turned, in a flash, on us all, and catches us messing up our lives the way we do. The next exhibit, though, focuses back on the legacy of greatness in the family. Indeed, this is the corner-stone of the collection. So, without further ado—

CHAPTER TWELVE

ABSOLUTELY FABIUS: vv. 13–8

- *cur Allobrogicis et magna gaudeat ara*
  natus in Herculeo Fabius lare, si cupidus, si
  uanus et Euganea quantumuis mollior agna,
  si tenerum attritus Catinensi pumice lumbum
  squalentis traducit auos emptorque ueneni
  frangenda miseram funestat imagine gentem? (vv. 13–18)

Why should a son find joy in **Allobrogics** and High Altar,
Born in the **Fabian** house, Hercules' shrine, if grasping, if
Inane, and soppier as you please than any *bien-né* **Venetian**
    lamb,
If rubbed down with pumice *Catinese*, all succulent tenderloin,
He puts unkempt forefathers on parade, and as The One who
    Purchased Poison
His likeness merits smashing, he casts a pall on the stricken
    clan?

Was **Numantinos** a generalizing plural? Was the general in question
Scipio Aemilianus, Africanus Minor? Or is this the same game, after the
Aemilii **Lepidi** (v. 9), with (some of) the same personnel, as at the start

50

in *Aemilianos* (v. 2)? As I mentioned, Scipio's natural brother, Fabius Aemilianus, accompanied him as a legate during his successful siege of Numantia in 134–133: the Scipiones hunted in pairs. Though Fabius won neither the triumph nor the name in Republican *history*, in his lobby, the father who named the Neronian *Fabius Numantinus* knew better.

In thus probing the triumphal name-fame Scipio-Fabius nexus, we slide without delay on into the fifth and last re-imagining of

• *Stemmata quid faciunt?*

before Juvenal is finally ready to declare his formula. For *Allobrogicis* (v. 13) at once echoes *Numantinos*, since it was Fabius Aemilianus' son Q. Fabius Maximus (*cos.* 121) who conquered the Gauls of Vienne and so won the triumphal *cognomen Allobrogicus*. No epic poet's roll-call of heroes could find an individual berth for *this* Fabius, by no stretch of the imagination the greatest of his clan: he signals that Juvenal means to explore the crowning glories of this *gens* in some detail.

Roll-call honours elsewhere fall to the Hannibalic **Fabius** Maximus *Cunctator*,[80] who was (for one thing) the Republic's last full *dictator* before the 'newspeak' perversions of Sulla and Caesar. The citation of *equitum cum dictatore magistros* (v. 8, perhaps in the company of *Fabricium*) already sent the mind racing back through the annals of Rome, where we would find the *Cunctator* emerging ennobled from the débâcle that besmirched both offices: in 217 after the disaster at Trasimene, appointed *mag. eq.* by the comitia, not picked by Fabius, M. Minucius Rufus overrode the defensive dilation; appointed the solecism of 'co-dictator', after an initial success Minucius needed Fabius and his son first to rescue, then to forgive him. Thereafter *dictatores* were only used for particular restricted administrative functions, and that only to the end of the war with Hannibal (202).[81]

It is worth pausing to take in the anxiety that the gaze of 'Slow-coach', the greatest of the Fabii Maximi, should generate in a well-brought-up Ponticus. Juvenal foregathers Fabii here to pile up maximum pressure, ready for the knock-out blow of the majestic maxim that follows.

Fabii[82] dominated long stretches of the proto-history of the Republic; they claimed descent from Hercules and a daughter of Evander,[83] and to derive from Remus' *Fabiani*, one of the two colleges of Luperci priests.[84] *Cunctator*'s great-grandfather was the first Fabius Maximus: Q. Rullianus (*coss.* V, 322–295, *dict.* II, *princeps senatus*), hero of the Samnite Wars;[85] grandfather was Q. Gurges (*coss.* III, 292–265, *princeps senatus*).[86]

To outdo them, was to become a human Christmas tree: *Q. Fabius Maximus Verrucosus Ouicula Cunctator* ('Quintus Fabius: The Greatest; Warty; Lambkin; Delayer') was destined and driven to become the Republic's most polyonymous hero, more than a match for (the sadly/proudly adoptive) *P. Cornelius Scipio Aemilianus Africanus Numantinus* we started from. The name-plate beneath Fabius Maximus' *imago*, a worn-out mass of misshapen prehistory glowering down ancestral disapproval, warts and all, can be imagined from his marble-plaque *Elogium* from the Forum of Augustus:

> *Q. Fabius] Q. f. Maximus, dictator bis, cos quinquiens, censor, interrex bis, aed. cur., q. bis, tr. mil. bis, pontif. aug. Primo consulatu Ligures subegit, ex iis triumphauit. Tertio et quarto Hannibalem compluribus uictoriis ferocem subsequendo coercuit. Dictator magistro equitum Minucio, quoius populus imperium cum dictatoris imperio aequauerat, et exercitui profligato subuenit et eo nomine ab exercitu Minuciano pater appellatus est. Consul quintum Tarentum cepit, triumphauit. Dux aetatis suae cautissimus et re<i> militaris peritissimus habitus est. Princeps in senatum duobus lustris lectus est.*[87]

Quintus Fabius Maximus, son of Quintus, Dictator twice, Consul five times, Censor, Interrex twice, Curule Ædile, Quaestor twice, Military Tribune twice, Priest, and Augur. In his first consulate, he subdued the Ligurians and held a triumph over them. In his third and fourth, he tied down Hannibal, on the rampage after a string of victories, by dogging his every move. As Dictator, he came to the rescue of Minucius, the Master of Horse, whose authority the Roman People had brought level to the dictator's authority, and to the rescue of his routed army, and on that account was saluted by Minucius' army as 'Father'. As Consul for the fifth time, he captured Tarentum and held a triumph. The doyen of his epoch, he was regarded as the canniest and most experienced in soldiering. He was chosen as Leader for the senate in two reviews.

What son *could* live up to that record? *Cunctator*'s boy did make it to the consulate; but then came a missing generation, before a double transfusion brought in new, adoptive blood: Q. Fabius Maximus Aemilianus (*cos.* 145) *and* Q. Fabius Maximus Seruilianus (*cos.* 142), whose sons were Q. Fabius Maximus Aemilianus Allobrogicus (*cos.* 121) and Q. Fabius Maximus Seruilianus Eburnus (*cos.* 126). Allobrogicus' grandson Q. Fabius Maximus was the Caesarian *triumphator de Hispanis* who managed to expire on the last day of his booby-prize *cos. suff.* in the last quarter of 45, but his sons became walking proofs of Augustan restoration, festooned with the over-bred names of Ae-milian-Cornelian Fabii: *Paullus* Fabius Maximus (*cos.* 11), Ovid's white hope and Princess Marcia's husband,[88] and *Africanus* Fabius Maximus (*cos.* 10). Paullus probably continued this re-living in the past, with a Fabia *Numantina* for daughter,[89] and Paullus Fabius *Persicus* for son (*cos.* 34CE, the last Fabian consulate; named for L. Aemilius Paullus Macedonicus' scalp, King *Perseus*:[90] Persicus' son was that priest of 59CE, Fabius Numantinus;[91] Claudius boasts bold on brass that:

> '(*non*) *paenitet Persicum, nobilissimum uirum amicum meum, inter imagines maiorum suorum **Allobrogici** nomen legere.*' (*Tabula Lugdunensis, col. II.* 24f.)[92]

> 'Persicus, that distinguished gent., my friend, does(n't) regret reading among the *imagines* of his ancestors the name "**Allobrogicus**".'

No post Julio-Claudian palace either could, or need, live up to these *ci-devant* aristocrats.[93] Emperors force home the lesson:

• 'What pedigrees do, is place intolerable psychic burdens on sons.'

Every Viceroy must precede a degenerate successor; vice sends people scuttling up the family tree to find the success now shamed.

So Juvenal has taken time out to detail a sad lot, the sad lot of 'The

Fabian Son': under Claudius, Fabius *Persicus* fell foul of imperial succession's changing of the guard.[94] Q. Fabius Maximus the son of Allobrogicus was debarred by the *praetor urbanus* of 99 from disposing of his patrimony, virtually 'disinherited' by the state—unless this was his father, 'as a youth the worst reprobate, but as an elder the most respectable luminary'.[95] 'Bobby-dazzler' *Eburnus* was 'named for his fair complexion', but (memorably) known as *Iouis pullus* ('catamite') because 'struck by lightning in the behind': true, when *censorius* (former censor), later in life (104), he killed his son out of hand in the privacy of the home, for unchastity, and was obliged to opt for a permanent sojourn overseas—or else (as another tradition has it) this was what his father did to him.[96] Earlier, Rullianus' juvenile delinquent son landed his *Gurges* label *a deuorato patrimonio* ('*Abyss*, from gulping down his inheritance'), in the bad old days before he became Leader of the House.[97]

Cunctator, too, proves how functional a father 'a [Fabian] pedigree makes for', and how dysfunctional a son. His son's career was, patently, *pater* pulling the strings, pulling *his* strings. In 217, he served under the *dictator*'s command; and in 216, at Cannae; in 215, he was *aed. cur.*, to his father, *cos. III*; in 214, he was *pr.* to daddy's *cos. IV*; in 213, finally, he was himself made *cos.*, but put in command of father's sphere of operations in the south: and *pater filio legatus* ('His father was on his son's staff'). The inevitable tale runs, that father rode past eleven out of twelve of the lictors before the son ordered the last lictor to order him to dismount: 'Then he finally did dismount, saying':

> . . . *tum demum desiliens, 'Experiri', inquit, 'uolui, fili, satin' scires consulem te esse (Liv. A. U. C. 24. 44. 9).*[98]

'I was just testing, son, to see if you knew you're consul.'

In this the year of The Son, Tarentum was lost: whereas his father's fifth and final consulate in 209 crowned his career, with a triumph for. . . regaining Tarentum.[99] From much earlier in the same story, feel *this* ton of authoritarian bricks from the patriot *pater*:

When his boy expressed satisfaction that the renegade *mag. eq.* had met his come-uppance, the greybeard shook his spear and tears spurted: 'you must erase the immaturity of those unpleasant words of yours. I'm not going to let citizens get rubbed out in my face, not within my reach [*ante ora manusque*]. . .. Son, get this from your father's long life. Have no hesitation or dubitation. Guard it safe. Nail it to the bottom of your heart for keeps: wrath aimed at the fatherland is blasphemy. In fact, no fouler sin is fetched down to the final darkness. Such has been the teaching of our elders, the teachings of old [*sic docuere senes*]. . .. Let's hurry to the rescue, *without* delay [*celeremus opem*]' (Sil. *Pun*. 7. 539–65)

This quintessential Fabian father buried his son (207–203)—whose own son would perish a mere *augur* in 196, before holding office (whereas grandfather was *augur* for sixty-two years). With grandson (probably) petered out the Dictator's direct line.[100] *Cunctator*'s great-hearted endurance of his son's decease was passed into the tradition by Cato the Elder, his 'spiritual son'.[101]

But every Fabius since 477 knew he had to be special, 'solitary and unique' in *uirtus* as his atavistic imperative commanded: the regiment of *imagines* stood, to eternity, for the collective suicidal patriotism that should run in the blood of every bearer of the name. *Fabii* plural[102] spelled, not a couple of brothers or a nuclear family, a couple of generations or the odd cousin (as with Scipiones), but the Roman version of the Spartan heroes wiped out at Thermopylae, with the crucial difference that one Fabian survivor remained to pass on the baton through all those scions down to Rullianus, and then on to Cunctator, to save Rome again and again: the story says by the Cremera 306 Fabii fought alone against all Veii, and died. The 'sole and unique' survivor was 'one' under-age Fabius left at home: without that boy, there could have been no fearsome *Cunctator* to be the 'one' to save Rome.[103] For the rest of time, every last Fabius learned on daddy's knee that they must live up to that boy who grew to defy total defeat in the Great War, single-handedly, *the dictator*.

This tall order bears the hallmark of myth: the mystification of unbearable mandates in blank mutual contradiction. The greatness of the 'Light Brigade' Fabii was their 'prompt/precipitate panache' (*quo ruitis, generosa domus?*),[104] which against Hannibal's generalship lost Flaminius Trasimene and then Varro Cannae, almost as disastrously as Cremera cost the clan. Yet as *his* forte, Fabius Maximus' *uirtus* enjoins stalling for your life.

So it is that precisely the same gentilician endowment spells both the devotional self-sacrifice of Fabii *en masse*[105] and *Cunctator*'s shifty living-to-fight-another-day. (As Appendix 3 will further explore.)

With *his* Fabius for cue, Juvenal brings his fusillade to maximum volume, to his acclamation of a *sola. . . atque unica uirtus* (v. 20). But he will continue onwards and upwards, to deafen every Ponticus for a further 255 lines of reverberation.

Still, in vv. 13–18, **Fabius** *is* given the full works. Not an easy club to join, all those masks looking over their spotty candidate. The *Satire* uses, not apostrophic miming, but energetic detailing to mould high modality into its distillation of gentilician mentality in its one, single, Fabius.

Fabius' triumphal heritage stretches away to the client nations of Gauls permanently attached to their conqueror's patronage in the cosmopolis, back to the first *Allobrogicus*, then on through an entire corridor of masks. All the Fabii bracketed between the Aemilian adoption and the primeval rutting of Hercules with Evander's daughter, memorialized in the foundation and eternal cult of his *Ara Maxima*, *quae maxima semper / dicetur nobis et erit quae maxima semper* ('the Greatest Altar, which we shall always call the Greatest Altar, and so it will be the Greatest Altar').[106] The tradition of Greatness written into the *hendiadys* (two phrases, one concept) between the triumphal *agnomen* and the holy shrine, the family hero and national *sanctum*, connects the origins to the last glories of the Republic, since at least the host of Fabii **Maximi**, from Rullianus through *Cunctator*, is engrossed in Juvenal's formula, which tellingly re-winds the annals back to the beginning of Roman time: *Allobrogicis et magna. . . ara.*[107] Any new Fabian pride-and-joy must know this story backwards.

The Son knew it before he was 'born, in the household protection of Hercules' divinity' (v. 14): here, the little family *lar* ('tutelary god of the household') is gargantuan as Mighty Hercules, who established the Great Altar that founded Rome as a centre for pious worship, the basic qualification of any city.[108] Time for another story: the mask of the *iuuenis* (youth) C. Fabius Dorsuo stares fixedly through his young descendant, warning of the clan's sacred destiny, to tread sedately and *un*hurriedly, looking to right or to left for neither friend for foe, on the holy path of religious duty, as *he* had done when passing through the investing Gauls from Capitol to Quirinal and back, *nihil ad uocem cuiusquam terroremue motus* ('utterly unmoved by anybody's words or attempt to frighten him'): through that *atrium* of *imagines*, then *eadem reuertens similiter constanti uultu graduque*... ('returning the same way, just the same, both expression and step held steady', Liv. *A. U. C.* 5. 46. 2f.). A model for all traffic to-and-fro from home to city to world (from *lar* to *urbs* to *orbis*).

Satire has its Fabian infant grow up in a conception all its own— blighted in tricolon:

[i]   *cupidus* (v. 14). No budding *Cunctator*, whose *uirtus* was founded on classic mastery of all the passions: *non hunc*. . . *superauerit umquam | inuidia aut*. . . *gloria*. . ., *non astus*. . . *non praeda aliusue cupido* ('Never ever mastered by anything, not by jealousy, vain-glory, cunning, booty, or any other desire').[109]

[ii] 'Oodles softer than a lambkin' (v. 15). Why? Because *Cunctator*'s gentle *comitas* and 'sheepish' *apragia* ('aversion from action') earned him, as a boy, the nickname *Ouicula*, which time knitted into a further badge of courage, distinguishing the hero's reserves of 'patient non-aggression', *quieta | mente capax*.[110] He is branded a *Euganea*n bell-wether as the hallmark of *nobilitas* (as if < [derived from] Greek *eugeneia*, 'noble birth').[111] He is *'oodles* softer', because as Fabius *Maximus* he would be (*quantum-uis*, 'as great as you please').

[iii] 'Erotically pumiced in the loins' (*attritus*, v. 16). This because 'attrition' of the enemy is the name of the fame-game of *Cuncta-tor*,[112] and his personal name was *Verrucosus*, for the 'wart' that grew over his stiff upper lip.[113] Nature had stamped the ancient

body with *moral* beauty: the *maiores* put (their) inner strength over (our) fetishized surfaces. The pumice must be '*Catinensi*an' because this toponym *could* have dubbed some 'rough-hewn *triumphator*' in the Punic Wars' battle-zone (*squalentis. . . auos*, v. 17); but in the post-lapsarian world it must brand-name some superior line in the electrolysis trade of pederastic skin-care.[114]

Juvenal has sketched his Fabius victim's growth from cradle to gambolling child (*agna*, 'lamb'), to pubescent sex-object (*tenerum*, 'tender'): his career finally twin-peaks in 'triumph' and 'funeral-ritual' (*traducit. . . funestat*, vv. 17–18). In these same images, he gets to stage a 'parade of forefathers, honest dirt under time's coating of dust', and profits from his patrimony to tot up the requisite 'death-count' of victims which always certified Roman triumph. Furthermore, 'traducing his dinosaur ancestors', he also 'frogmarches them as filthy prisoners in his triumph'; and, 'filing past the rough-hewn *imagines*', he shows them off to his audience. But then he 'brings shame on the family', and his (social) 'death plunges the funereal *imagines* into mourning', enlisted for the ceremonial parade to the forum (cf. *squalentis*, v. 17: 'in mourning for the dead/for shame'). Where there should have been the 'joy' of family pride (*gaudeat*, v. 13), our parody Fabius, himself as 'emptily vain' and 'vainly empty' (*uanus*, v. 15) as any *atrium*'s waxwork mask (*imagine*, v. 18), profanes the Fabii, his sacred inheritance (*ara. . . lare*, vv. 13–14), and winds up in this matching hendiadys of 'degraded caricature and shattering pollution' (. . . -*que*. . ., v. 17 ~ [= responds with]. . .*et*. . ., v. 13), which spells the ultimate nadir of 'clan misery' (*miseram. . . gentem*, v. 18).

For this latest protégé has 'bought poison' (v. 17),[115] and 'killed his family'. Whether his poison would be for a mark or a mistress, for himself or some rich uncle, or what, doesn't matter. In whichever case, the smear says, just one solitary wickedness from a Fabius kills off centuries of fame.

Far from living up to the Fabii Maximi, this Son kills them off before himself becoming a father or 'grandfather', let alone a 'forefather' (*auos*, v. 17): he mortifies the *gens* with the disgrace of his own *imago*, which were 'better in smithereens', the way a public enemy's deserved to be treated (*frangenda. . . imagine*, v. 18).[116] The artists made the waxwork figures live, the descendant kills the dead—dead.[117]

Summed up in the loving caricature of this Little Lord Fauntleroy is the role cast by the satirist for his pilot-audience of *Ponticuses*: 'you' (*incip-is*, v. 11) are a child; a lamb; jail-bait; every Lady's Son. And Satire's poison pen has turned the intimate intricacies of family fame on the victim, put down as cowardly; unmanned; Hercules-turned-poisoner. How far from gladdening globe-trotting, barbarian-bashing deeds of derring-do can Juvenal write this Roman game of making a name for yourself? Quite a haul of blame for him, resolutely libellous on the obsoletely nebulous.

The Fabian fantasia climbs to a *poetic* climax of thought-bodied-as-word in the splendidly depressive display of its sonorous final Golden Line (a verse that consists of two epithets paired up with their nouns and flanking the verb that links/separates them): *frangenda miseram funestat imagine gentem* (v. 18). In this grim gem we savour the *gravamen* of degeneracy – the defiled displacement of the eugenic gen in *magna gaudeat ara* and *Euganea. . . agna* (vv. 13, 15).

• *Stemmata quid faciunt?*

• 'Turn Juvenal loose on aristocracy, and what can he come up with? He'll knock the stuffing out of degeneracy, what else?'

CHAPTER THIRTEEN

COURAGE, MON BRAVE: vv. 19-20

tota licet ueteres exornent undique cerae
atria, nobilitas sola est atque unica uirtus. (vv. 19–20)

FOR ALL that antique casts top off perfection all around—
WHOLE HALLS full—yet Nobility is *non pareil*, inimitable,
    when it means Virtue.

• 'Pedigrees, now, what's their game?'

Juvenal's answer gathers together the full momentum built up in that
fivefold chain of interrogation: that is what it comes out and *tells* us.
Juvenal has 'decked out whole halls-full of traditional images of gen-
tilician ancestry whose *imagines* together represent the name-fame-
word-echo-statue-figure-imagery of the Roman Tradition' (vv. 19f.).

Here, too, Juvenal still re-cites canonical text: to 'puff' Virtue, he
quotes from the teachings of Ovid's authoritative Professor of Whore-
dom, Madam Dipsas' instruction 'not to be fooled by antique casts
around halls—Tell the young man without funds to take himself off
with his grandsires' (Ov. *Am.* 1. 8. 65f. : *nec te decipiant ueteres circum*
atria cerae, / tolle tuos tecum, pauper amator, auos). As he proclaims,
he has been 'decking out' with rhetorical amplification (*exornatio*) the
'wax-tablet' *of his own text* (*cerae*), by re-writing the venerable classics'

60

celebration of cultural kudos into a line-up of Roman Antiquity (*ueteres. . . undique*).

And as he pulls his argument together, Juvenal now cashes out his series of plurals disestablishing singleness: the prior occupation of the ephebe's identity by myriad ancestors, before he can set about fashioning one of his own; the binding power of fame handed down through the patriarchal name; the Roman family image-repertoire of art-lined ante-chambers (*tota. . . atria, ueteres. . . cerae*; *exornent*: the imaginary, façade, icing, appearance). All, we have seen, set to dominate the need to isolate the 'sole and unique', to integrate the 'sole-'n'-unique' individuality, to bring the prodigal back to the family fold (*sola. . . atque unica*; *est*: the real, substance, cake, truth).

As the poet reaches this, his poem's first base, his writing even mimetically re-presents on the page its own prooemial role as 'gateway' porch leading to the rest of its domain:

| *TOTA. . .*
| *ATRIA. . .*

Every word of every line similarly parades Juvenal's vision of growing up in Rome as the Son's passing to and fro under the gaze of expropriating Ancestors' death(ly) masks. To terrorize his *homunculus* with The Past, Juvenal gathers all the metropolis's mansions into one happy hunting-ground, as 'unique' as a Fabius should be, after Cremera, since Trasimene.[118]

The 'formula' he slams down is the Noble Lie that hectors Ponticus toward its goal:

nobilitas sola est atque unica uirtus.

The sluggingly simple and sweeping stuff of Plain Truth, this—with a vengeance. Yet generations of pupils have needed saving from *total* mis-reading. By Duff: '**virtus** is subject, **nobilitas** is predicate'. Or by Courtney: 'VIRTUS is the subject, NOBILITAS SOLA ATQUE UNICA. . . the predicate'. No, the pay-off for Juvenal's review of gentilician Rome is *not* that

Noble birth constitutes manliness.

61

Rather,

Virtue is the only nobility worthy of the name.

But saving readers from error is not the only game in town. Juvenal is taking the *greatest* care to show up in his syntax how utterly both these master-terms, *nobilitas* and *uirtus*, depend on context for meaning. They intertwine in their 'inimitable uniqueness' so neatly that their aphorism even reads happily as one emphatically re-doubled predicate awaiting a subject still to arrive with the next verse:

e.g.: [*est*] *nobilitas sola atque unica uirtus / [pietas].*

The sole nobility and only virtue is [respectfulness].

The release of that last word, *uirtus*, which has been jacked up higher with every word that precedes, in the outcome carries only a spurious, formal finality. So far, we're scarcely the wiser for it.

Consider the tag this way:

• 'Would it get the approval of Scipio-Aemilius-Fabius?'

Answer:

• 'Yes. And in whichever sense they might read it, too.'[119]

For *any* authority-figure could recommend both *nobilitas* as the essence of *uirtus* and *uirtus* as the essence of *nobilitas*. These grand items bespeak 'logonomic blueprints' rather than simply naming ideals, let alone operating referentially.[120] That is to say, mouthing the watch-word *sounds* high-minded enough, but we'll need coordinates if we are to see what stake it puts up, in what discourse. These slogans tell us to regulate our behaviour according to a code.

Satire has been providing one major context for meaning here: a sharp put-down for the nobs was a fair expectation before he got started.[121] But now that Juvenal has shamed his victim by invoking the traditional protreptic of the *mos maiorum* on his high horse, he has thickened the plot. Now that his writing has invoked so much of the repertoire of the classical canon, his poem must ask, even as it lays down the law, what construction its readers think they can put on traditional values; and what deconstruction their currency as wisdom merits. Is Roman history, in its traditional respect for aristocratic respect for the Elders, all just antiquated lumber and banal cliché?

- 'What goes when *stemmata* go?'

Juvenal sounds *so* much like that traditional hoary figure, the Elder Cato, a Curius, a Fabricius, or any of the other Roman Fathers from *Cunctator* to Fabius Servilianus: those gleaming loins of Juvenal's pumiced Fabius (v. 16) are not *his* story, but Tradition's story-name-infamy-*imago* of that Fabius *Eburnus*, nicknamed *Iouis pu[e]llus* (remember?) and blotted from the escutcheon by his father, at the cost of liquidating his branch of the line.

Setting your teeth against degeneracy is not the preserve of upstarts and rebels, it is the archetypal stock-in-trade of 'aristocratic' ideology.[122] Therefore the real issue for Juvenal, if he would ever deal with anything so real as an issue, is rather:

- 'Can moral discourse function after all the centuries? Or is it condemned to re-play heirloom saws, an overload of tralatician uplift beyond repair?'

To see where the argument so far has taken us, Juvenal's Hall of Fame must hold up the traffic passing in and out of Roman palaces for awhile yet, and show us how post-Republican Rome might think usefully, and joke tellingly, with its incubus of Noble Virtues imaged in Virtuous Nobles.

In Juvenal's second century, Cornelii Scipiones were defunct and Fabii Maximi long gone. Their moth-balled myths live(d) on, indispensable to think with.

- *Stemmata quid faciunt?*

- 'The myth of the Republican phylogram (kin-structure) marked out the terrain for discussion of nobility and virtue in all their myriad colourings.'

This cultural factor hands Satire its greatest hold over the present, as the deplorably entropic deterioration of the past.

CHAPTER FOURTEEN

LLOYD'S NAMES: vv. 21–38

*Paulus uel **Cossus** uel **Drusus** moribus esto,*
hos ante effigies maiorum pone tuorum,
praecedant ipsas illi te consule uirgas.

prima mihi debes animi bona.

                    sanctus haberi
iustitiaeque tenax factis dictisque mereris?   25

*agnosco procerem: 'salue **Gaetulice**, seu tu*
***Silanus**, quocumque alio de sanguine rarus*
ciuis et egregius patriae contingis ouanti' —
exclamare libet populus quod clamat Osiri
inuento.

                    quis enim generosum dixerit hunc qui   30
indignus genere et praeclaro nomine tantum
insignis?

nanum cuiusdam Atlanta uocamus,
Aethiopem Cycnum, prauam extortamque puellam
Europen; canibus pigris scabieque uetusta
leuibus et siccae lambentibus ora lucernae   35
nomen erit pardus, tigris, leo, si quid adhuc est
quod fremat in terris uiolentius.

                                                                ergo cauebis
et metues ne tu sic **Creticus** *aut* **Camerinus.** (vv. 21–38)

Paulus, Cossus, Drusus. . .—become one of them, with their traits;
Put *those* before your family ancestor portraits;
Let *them* clear the way for the magistrate's parade of power,
    lined-up for a consul like you.

First thing you owe me: goodness of mind.

                                                        Regarded as 'a saint,
He never gave up on Right'—are you worth that, what you do, all
    you say?   25

I spot some High-up: 'Greetings, **Gaetulicus**—or you're a
Silanus, whatever other bloodline you're from—citizen
Extraordinaire, that cut above the rest, acclaimed blessing on your
    country.'
— I want to shout loud what the folk shout for Osiris
Found.

    You see, whoever's going to say someone has breeding who 30
No way matches the breed, and the name, fairest of fair, is the
    only way
He stands out?

            Someone's dwarf, giant 'Atlas' we call him;
Their Nigerian's the original snowy 'Swann'; that no-good,
    disfigured girl is

65

'Miss Beau Monde'; or a pack, now, gone to sloth, through
   chronic mange
Bare of coat, dogs licking oil-lamp's face-grease dry as a bone: 35
For name they'll be 'Panther', 'Tiger', 'Lion'. . . or whatever's yet
   to come,
Roaring anywhere on earth more savagely still.

                                        That is why you'll take care,
And fret—is this you? called '**Creticus**', or called '**Camerinus**', just
   so,
—but called it how? *Like that?*   38

Juvenal has spoken. In what will prove to room-divide the *entrée* clean
in two between *tota. . . atria,* i.e. at

   cerae / atria (vv. 1–18/19 – 19/20–38).[123]

To get there we passed in reading through the *fauces* (door-way /
jaw-way) of his house of verse; now we bow and scrape our way out
again. There will be the same ingredients as before,[124] but the emphasis
will shift as Juvenal moves outside the *atrium.*

   His hectoring 'questions' continue where they left off (vv. 24f.,
30–2). He works from the trappings of the pedigree some more (*effigies
maiorum. . . tuorum, genere et praeclaro nomine,* vv. 22, 31). He
presents the topic as 'supreme' (*prima mihi,* v. 24), a vital matter of
'values and worth' (*debes, sanctus. . . iustitiaeque tenax. . . mereris,
indignus,* vv. 24f., 31). And he lines up more idealized anxiety-figures
(*Paulus. . . Cossus. . . Drusus; Silanus; Camerinus,* vv. 21, 27, 38),
featuring fresh triumphal titles (*Gaetulicus, Creticus,* vv. 26, 38).
Further scornful address is deferred until the re-start (*Rubelli / Blande,*
vv. 39f.), but is the *subject* of this sermon. For *uirtus* is emphatically
pictured as in the gift of those who assess its parade.

   The lecture begins from Three Golden Rules of positive protreptic
(*moribus esto. . ., v. 21; pone. . ., v. 22; praecedant. . ., v. 23*), visualizes
a successful climb to 'the top' (*te consule,* v. 23), and enjoins 'the highest
aspirations in town' (*rarus / ciuis et egregius,* vv. 27f.). But 'acclaim'

(*ouanti*, / *exclamare*, vv. 28f.) at once gives way to undermining insult (/ *indignus* cancels / *insignis*, vv. 31f.),[125] as the aristocratic *nomen* is turned over, and under the token we find—nothing; or even less.

Instead, an unsettling parade of the abjected other files past: 'pet dwarf' freakshow, a stare at the exotic imported 'black'. The slide down-market steepens, so meet the reject sex-object: 'bad' means 'maimed, of *girls*'; and, low as you can get, 'dogs run to fat, overtaken by the mange and hairless. The only face *they* lick dry belongs to the candle' (vv. 32–5).[126] Finally, *nomen* in the maw of Satire becomes 'the roar of a great cat—or anything on earth you can think more violent' (vv. 36f.): Juvenal is 'warning' his terrorized addressee, 'watch out and tremble' before him as you would before a true Roman Father. 'Or else' (vv. 37f.). You are *given* your name, he insists, and you may get landed with. . . something *horrid* (v. 38). Even if you hear yourself called something nice, it may only mark how horrid you really are.

So the victim is put in charge of his destiny only to put him at the mercy of others. First he is told to live up to the *mores* of three primeval names-for-fame which have it in common both that they were all proudly revived by the early Julio-Claudian élite, and that each of them began as a gentilician *cognomen* but, in a short-lived aristocratic onomastic fashion, re-located as *praenomina*.[127]

[i]   *Paulus*, as we have been reminded (between *Aemilianos* and *Fabius*, vv. 2, 14), straddles L. *Aemilius* Paullus Macedonicus with Paullus *Fabius* Maximus.[128]

[ii] *Cossus* stays within one *gens*, covering A. *Cornelius* Cossus (*cos.* 428), one of the three heroes to win the *spolia opima* and as such, presumably the Cossus (not) left in silence by Virgil's Anchises,[129] and the Augustan Cossus *Cornelius Lentulus* (*cos.* 1),[130] whose conquests in Africa bestowed the triumphal name *Gaetulicus*, though without the triumph, on his son and descendants, as we are soon prompted to recall (v. 26).

[iii] Lastly, *Drusus*. As we will soon be reminded (*alto Drusorum stemmate*, v. 40, the lofty pedigree of the Drusi'), this is a long-ago title, won in a duel from a champion-chieftain Gaul *Drausus*.[131]

The name passed, through Livia (Drusilla) Augusta, from the Republican *Liuii* Drusi into imperial dynastics. From her younger son *Nero Claudius* Drusus, with its own promotion of Nero from *cognomen* to *praenomen*, to Tiberius Caesar's son's prepositive Drusus *Caesar*, as well as still appended to the long titles of Gaius, Claudius and Nero. As a sign of royalty, it gained extra signification even when still a traditional *cognomen*, advertising the pedigree of Livia's Scribonian step-brother *Libo* Drusus from the *Liuii* Drusi.[132]

Juvenal's invitation to live up to any of these names in your *mores* includes both the idea of emulating Republican *exempla*—of imitating their lives, not just lifting their names. Later figures, from what is *now* ancient history, have themselves already faced the challenge, to live up to the titles without their precluding them from making a mark of their own.

The Augustan/Tiberian trio all 'put these persons' <names> '*in front of* their ancestral *names*': the victim is next told to do the same, not, that is, to take on their names, but 'to reproduce the *mores* they (are to) stand for'; 'to prefix these names-that-bespeak-*mores* on the *tituli* before your ancestors' *imagines*', 'to set up an installation of famous moral characters to block out your family *imagines*, and let *mores* blot out *maiores*'; 'to value what these worthies stand for above your pedigree' (v. 22).[133]

In this dense realization of the imagery of '*anter*iority', he continues, 'when you have made it to the consulate, those ancestors of yours can march *ahead of* your *fasces*'. Or, 'once you have prized *mores* above ancestral *imagines*', don't stop, but carry on and 'let those old names march ahead of your *fasces* when you are consul'; 'give these chosen models of goodness priority over the very lines of your stemma when you are consul' (v. 23).[134] 'The first requirement', however, is for 'excellence of the mind'. And this is Juvenal's first construal of *uirtus* (v. 24).

Ancestors came 'before' Romans temporally: they *can* only 'precede' them; but concretely they 'went before' when the *imagines* were taken out of the *atrium* in the moving family-tree column, and preceded the corpse to the *forum* for his funeral encomium. And imaginarily, they are always 'arrayed *in front of* their descendant', because their line-up *confronts* him whenever he comes in his front door, and stretches *ahead of* him whenever he ventures forth into the world from the *domus*. The *imagines* crowd the foyer precisely to get in first and (pre-)occupy the self. Like spirit lictors, they are there to shoo distracting or obstructive interference from the way ahead. So in these (moralized) 'ancestors' are imaged 'the *uirtus* of the mind' which Juvenal preaches.

The point is to *choose* a model of goodness (*uel . . . uel*, v. 21): then virtue can be construed on the (traditional) lines of (an adjusted) 'nobility'. 'Excellence of the mind' is still the same business of imaginative representation of idealized anxiety-figures to the self as ever *uirtus* was for the unfortunate Sons of severe Republican Fathers.

The charge of the harangue, however, is already tilting away from the aspiring youth striding to and fro in his waiting-room, re-imagining as best he can the cabinets of masks, the portraiture and statuary as the best character-forming models that ethics can recommend. For this goodness is 'in my book, an obligation', and it's 'owing to me' (v. 24). If 'you' want 'the reputation' of a moral character (*haberi*, v. 24), you must 'earn' it, 'by what you do as by what you say' (*factis dictisque*, v. 25). And *that* is a question of entering sociality, 'where you speak to and are spoken of, where your deeds interact with others', 'where more people than yourself put into words what you do, and what you say does things to your fellows'. Thus, both *sanctus* and *haberi* are passives; and *mereris* is a middle. Being 'blessed' requires worshippers; 'tenacious pursuit of justice' calls for public performance in and out of court, for forensic performance in the disputatious home of wrangling, vitriolic invective, character-assassination.

The satirist is ready to single out the would-be 'aristocrat of the soul', in a social setting: they all want 'recognition' as such (*agnosco procerem*, v. 26). When grandees step toward and out of their doors, dependants queue to greet them, at the morning *salutatio*. This means, precisely, getting the name right: Juvenal doesn't care what 'your' name is.

He shows this by not bothering whether 'you' come before his gaze as a Cornelius Lentulus **Gaetulicus**, or as an adoptive Iunius **Silanus** Gaetulicus,[135] and so the bearer of the traditional sign of both in-bred snobbery and the exercise of 'choice' in the fashioning of the family name-fame-future – an (early) imperial version of those *Aemiliani* of the Republic.[136] By ruling out any difference between one clan, whether under a 'triumphal' ticket, 'or' if it goes by a name which may or may not indicate the same clan (*seu*), or 'no matter what other blood-line' (*quocumque alio de sanguine*), the writing cancels out the generous offer of free choice the victim was handed at first.[137]

Instead, this big name 'rarity' is firmly saddled with the age-old leveller of Roman *libertas*. He is a *ciuis*, a single *procer* whose highest achievement would be to devote singular service to the 'father*land*' (vv. 26–8). Fame calls for the citizen-body's 'mass-acclamation' of 'one who stands out in a crowd' (*ouanti, e-gregius*, v. 28). Until the *populus* 'finds' the resurrected Saviour Osiris and shouts its communal joy (in Greek it would be: *heurêkamen, sugchairomen*, vv. 29f., 'Our find, our joy'), there is no miracle. So the same rule operates wherever the World State stretches, from the metropolis all the way to the East, both in the old *ciuitas*, and wherever Isis travels—as impossibly miraculous as the way that Juvenal can hear in *ouanti* / the sacred joy of Osiri / inuento.

The judgement of the *patria* and *populus* next transforms into 'anyone'. Anyone who asks themself 'if a noble with a noble name gets a name for nobility <or not>' (vv. 30– 2).[138] This questioning of the right to bear a famous name is the natural condition of language, which is made up of all the names 'we all decide to hang on whatever we do' (*uocamus*, v. 32). The plurality of discourse adds together all those individual 'votes' (*quis. . . dixerit*, v. 30). If 'nobility' depends, not on genes, but on recognition, this is because it is discriminated by dint of language (*nomine*, v. 31).

This menacing build-up leads to the nasty outburst of prejudice and disgust which gives victim *Ponticus*es the works: 'we', each and every single and unique one of us, know that words negotiate social relations. In dictionaries, they say and mean what they mean and say; but in use, language is only exceptionally representable as doing any such thing— and then, *caueat auditor* ('Watch out, reader').[139]

70

In Juvenal, for example, discussion of *uirtus* cannot help but provide an opportunity to play at 'looking back' in anger. When Satire comes out and tells us (satirists) that words can euphemize, the words he uses dysphemize. When Juvenal endows his scabby thane with all the brute terror of a 'Lionheart—or pick something with a louder roar'—he does the opposite. He rips apart the security of all who feel secure in praise from their fellow-creatures.

Far from merely mouthing some platitude about 'goodness', or picking a favourite hero, Juvenal's pupil must 'watch out', somehow or other, and 'dread'—his syntax. He writes: *ne tu sic. . . aut* (v. 38). 'You. . . See? You. . .'. You must 'fear that you might be (called, given the name, entitled) some big name or another *on these terms*'. He obliges us readers/reciters to name the verb ourselves: 'If "we" call you a Lord, you might be being euphemized. Or you might be being mock-euphemized. You might actually be being dysphemized. Indeed, you might be being *satirized*.' It doesn't matter *which* famous name you choose, again, for Juvenal is beating genealogy with a much bigger stick.

We saw that even our generous range of heroes, *Paulus*, *Cossus* and *Drusus*, are paradigmatically ambivalent, as those who would live up to the names melodramatized their imitativeness but to varying degrees achieved little else, or less. And now, of these latest examples, *Creticus* is a triumphal name which might spell unofficial acclamation or general sarcasm, or might spell official investiture—and general glee. *Camerinus*, on the other hand, might liken you to those bluest-blooded Sulpicii, like *Galba*, and (experts say) it might make you another Coruncanius, and a frugal plebeian to match *Curius* and *Fabricius*.[140] *But*, if Crete is where liars tell us they are all liars, and, besides, *Creticus* names a breed of hunting-hound, well then Camerium was scrubbed from the map of Roman Italy aeons ago, back in protohistory, so these complimentary names, for all their *bona fide* heraldics and their (more or less) exemplary call to emulation, are no less a pair of gift-horses than. . . was *Ponticus* to name/compliment/insult the target of this proem with.

Romans well knew that their *cognomina* (and some of their *nomina*) bespoke failings and defects, without euphemism. Father was cruel to be kind, getting in before Son was hurt by insult and nickname.[141] Or was that his nomothetic *pleasure*? Worse, Son might be saddled with the mockery for his *Father*'s deformity or depravity. In the arena of public, civic discourse, *fama* turned on the logic of *inuidia*, according to which 'infamy' is co-existent and co-extensive with 'fame'. Hatred of looking up to *any* superior being means that any thought along the lines of 'They've really got it in for me' spells grudging respect. The only variety in town.

Such has been the story in Juvenal's Hall of Fame:

[i] *Aemiliani*, first: the adoptive lie to fix up sterility, then shout it to eternity (v. 3).

[ii] *Numantini, Allobrogici, Gaetulicus, Creticus* and *Drusus*, next: triumphantly declaring the conqueror to belong among his barbarians, under his protective wing as he becomes one of them, their tribal chieftain.[142]

[iii] *Coruinus* names divine glory, to be imaged in a scare-crow's familiar, the absurdist crow on his crown (v. 5).[143]

[iv] *Camerinus* lends its blend of Antiquity with extinction (v. 38).

[v] *Lepidi, Paulus, Blandus, Capito, Pansa, Natta, Dolabella, Verres, Lateranus, Brutus, Lentulus, Vindex, Cicero, Cocles* will typify the proud scars of the traditional *cognomen*, live evil animating/dogging the cultural poetics of power at Rome.[144]

Roman Satire inhabits and animates Roman discourse like a virus that poisons as it inoculates the body politic.

• 'Dickens, but non-fiction?'

CHAPTER FIFTEEN

ALL THE WAY, ALLWAYS: TRANSLATION OF JUVENAL, *SATIRE* 8. 39–275[145]

Who was *that* sermon for? It's you I'm talking to, **Rubellius
Blandus.** You're puffed up with the high-faluting pedigree of the
    Drusi, as though   40
You'd done something yourself for which you'd be noble,
So that you'd be the child of a woman resplendent with the blood
    of **Iulus,**
Not a hireling who does weaving below the huff and puff of the
    embankment.
'You peasants', you say, 'lowest fraction of our mob,
Not one of you can pinpoint where your father was born,   45
Whereas I—*I* am a Cecropid.' Live your life, from this parentage
Derive lasting joy. Still, right at the bottom of the Roman masses
You'll find the eloquent citizen: from the masses who wear the
    toga will come   48a+49b
The one to take legal knots and riddles in the statutes and solve
    them.   50
It's from here that a young man heads for the Euphrates, or the
    Dutch reservation
Legionary garrison, indefatigable in combat; while you—

Zero, apart from being a Cecropid, spitting image of a Herm
  that's been nobbled.
In fact the only criterion you come out ahead on is that
Herm has a marble head, whereas the cast of you is alive.   55
Tell me this, Child of the Trojans: with dumb beasts,
Who would rate any of them good stock if they're not brave? For
  sure the flying
Racehorse gets our praise this way, the one with most wins, that
  gets
Victory fired up and cock-a-hoop, the prize a push-over, applause
  willing, arena booming;
That horse is the noble one, whatever the grass it comes from,
  whose   60
Start dashes into a clear lead, and its dust is out in front on the
  track.
But off to market goes the beast sired by Coryphaeus or
Hirpinus, if too seldom Victory alights on the chariot's yoke.
Zero respect for ancestors there: no credit is given
For dead shades; they're told to swap masters for sums that are 65
Tiny, they pull the harness with worn-out necks
Because they're slow-coaches fit only to turn the mill, never mind
  their grandsires.
Therefore, so we may admire you, and not what you have, give
  me something specific
That I can engrave on your record, apart from the glories
That we award and awarded, to the ones you owe
  everything to.   70

That's quite enough for a youth whose reputation comes down to
  us
As proud, puffed up, up to here with his close relatedness to
  Nero.
Not commonly found, you know, is care for the community—not
  in *that*

74

Lucky state. But the idea that your worth should be set at the
glory of your family,
That's something, **Ponticus**, I'd reject on the terms that you'd do
nothing yourself   75
To produce glory to come. It's pitiful to rely on the reputation of
others,
In case there is a collapse and the roof falls in once the pillars are
removed.
The vine-shoot trailed on the ground longs for some partner-less
elms.
Do be a good soldier, a good guardian, and, yes, an adjudicator
Beyond corruption; if ever you're summoned to testify in some
dodgy   80
And murky case, even if Phalaris commands you to give
False witness and dictates your perjury with his bull fetched in
and ready,
Just see you believe it the highest sin to put breathing before your
honour,
And for the sake of life to ruin the reasons for living.
To deserve death is to be dead, even if dinner is a hundred
oysters   85
From Gaurus and the bath's filled right up with *Cosmus*.

Long-awaited your province has been: when finally you
Are welcomed as governor, set your vexation within limits,
And your greed, too. Have pity on allies who lack funds—
You see the bones of all they have sucked dry of vanished
marrow.   90
Keep in your sights what the laws preach, what the senate
authorizes,
The great rewards in store for the good, the way a thunderbolt
fair and square
Toppled both **Capito** and **Tutor** with condemnation from the
house,

Plunderers of Cilician pirates. Yet what compensation does
    condemnation bring?
A receiver, Chaerippus: look out for one to handle your tatters, 95
When **Pansa** robs you of whatever **Natta** left you with;
And hush now: it's crazy to throw away your ferry-money on top
    of everything else.

No, it wasn't the same whinging in the old days and the damage
    wasn't half
As bad a wound when the allies were prosperous, i.e. recently
    subdued.
Then every home bulged: there stood tall a vast heap   100
Of cash, a Spartan cape, royal purple from Cos,
Along with Parrhasius' paintings and Myron's statues,
There was living ivory by Phidias, not to mention Polyclitus'
Plentiful output of work all over the place, and scarcely a table
    short of some Mentor.
From there **Dolabella**, from here **Antony**, from there   105
Verres the temple-robber took back on their soaring galleons
Hushed-up loot, for plenty of triumphs over peace—more than in
    war.
Nowadays the allies have a few teams of oxen, a modest troop of
    mares,
But these'll be stripped from them, even the sire of the herd, on
    seizure of the property,
To be joined by the actual household spirits, if any image is
    worth a look.   110
Maybe the Rhodians are useless in war, and Corinth is drenched
    in perfume?   113
Well, you can despise them, quite right, too: young men coated in
    bodyhair-remover,
A whole nation's smooth calves, what are they going to do to
    you?   115
Bristling Spain, though, you should keep well away from, and
    Gaulish latitudes,

Ditto the flank of Illyria; let off, as well, those reapers
Who cram Rome when it takes time out for the circus and theatre:
How big will your pay-off be for such appalling guilt,
When it's not long since **Marius** debagged the Africans, until they
    were skin-t?   120
Care must be taken, as a first principle, that no grave wrong be
    done
To those who are both brave and wretched. You may remove all
    there is anywhere
That is gold or silver, but you'll still leave behind shields and
    swords.   123
What I just stated is no *dictum*, it's the truth: 125
Trust me, everyone, I'm reading you leaves from the Sibyl's Book
    of Revelations.

If you have a company of saints for your staff, if no person
Chevelu puts your justice up for sale, if there are no charges
    against your wife,
And along your circuit, through all the townships, her hooked
Claws aren't getting ready to tour and swoop on cash *à la*
    Celaeno the Harpy,   130
Then you may indeed count back your ancestry from Picus on
    down, and if you
Are turned on by elevated names, then take the whole
    Titanomachic shooting-match,
And stick them among your ancestors, with Prometheus
    himself.   133
But if ambition and lusty caprice hustle you away
    head-over-heels,   135
If you snap cane after cane in pools of allied blood, if you
Are turned on by tiring lictors out and blunting their axes,
Then there starts to weigh against you your very forefathers'
Nobility, holding up their bright torch before your shame.
Every spiritual flaw harbours a more conspicuous guilt   140

Within itself, in proportion with the greatness accorded the
    sinner.
What's it to me that you have been a persistent signatory to
    forged deeds
In temples that your grandfather built, with your father's statue
    over your shoulder,
Awarded for his triumph? What's that worth, if you screw around
    after dark,
Hiding your forehead under the cover of an imported *Santones*
    hood?   145

Past his ancestors' ashes and bones, flying
In his buggy, zooms fatty **Lateranus**. And no one else,
None but he, bites the wheel with the brake: the mule-driver
    consul.
Yes, it's night-time; but still, the Moon sees, and, to bear witness,
    the stars
Strain their eyes. When the period of office is   150
Finished, in broad daylight **Lateranus** will grip
The whip, not for a moment will he worry about bumping into a
    friend
Now a senior citizen. No, he'll get in first with a nod of the cane,
    then unbundle
The fodder and tip it all out for his exhausted animals.
Meantime, though fleecy victims and a ruddy bull-calf   155
Are his sacrifice, **Numa**-style, the oath he takes before Jove's altar
He swears by Epona alone, by the portraits painted beside the
    stinking stables.
But when he chooses to renew the all-night festivities of the
    tavern,
Out to meet him comes the Syro-Phoenician drenched constantly
    with perfume,
At the double, a Syro-Phoenician resident of the *Idumaean*
    Gate,   160
Playing the keen host, with 'Lord and King' for his greeting,

78

Plus skirts-up Cyane with her carafe and her prices.

The apologist for guilt will tell me, 'We did that, yes, we too,
When we were youths.' O.K. But you sure quit, and no further
Nursed your bad habit. Keep short the ugly adventures
    you have;   165
Let some of your felonies get trimmed off with your first beard.
Go soft and let off boys: **Lateranus** is off to those
Tankards at the Baths, off where the awnings carry ads.,
Although his maturity is ripe for war and so preserving
    Armenia's, and Syria's,
Rivers, not forgetting the Rhine-Danube. Keeping **Nero**   170
Safe can be delivered by physiques his age. Send to Ostia, **Caesar**,
Send off, but hunt out your governor in a mighty. . . tavern:
You'll find him with some hit-man or other, reclining,
In a mêlée of sailors—thieves—runaway slaves,
In between hangmen and cardboard-coffin-makers,   175
Some flat-out eunuch-priest Gallus' tambourine, on hold.
Here's the equality of freedom—shared glasses, all-purpose couch
Just the same for all, no table kept separate for anyone.
What would you do, **Ponticus**, if you'd landed this sort of slave?
I know it, off to furthest Lucania or your workhouse in Etruria
    you'd pack him.   180
But you lot, those Born of Troy, you go light on yourselves.
    Things
That foul a tinker will grace **Volesuses** or a **Brutus**.

But what if there's never so much muck, so much shame,
In the examples I put to work, that there aren't yet worse to
    come?
Once your assets were finished off, Damasippus, you hired out
    your voice   185
For panto, so you could act Catullus' *The Ghost* and howl the
    place down.
Laureolus was actually a hit when played with **Lentulus'** dash,

But, if I'm the critic, it qualifies him for crucifixion—for real.
  And, no, don't
Forgive the Roman People; this People wears a face too brazen
  for that,
Sat watching members of the aristocracy perform in
  multi-farce,   190
Listening to comic routines from **Fabii**, able to laugh at
Knock-about by **Mamerci**. The pay-off for selling their 'deaths'
Doesn't signify, does it? They take the pay under no compulsion
  from **Nero**,
They don't pause about taking the pay at the high praetor's
  games.
Still and all. Imagine the chopping-block is set *this* side, so, and
  the stage on *that*:   195
Which to prefer? Has anyone shuddered at death so badly that
  he'd be
Thymele's *jaloux*, associate of Corinthus the clown?
Still. He's no miracle when the Emperor is a harpist, that ham
From the nobility. Beyond this, what's left but training to be a
  gladiator? And, there, you have the disgrace of Rome on your
  hands: in no Gaul's armour,   200
Fighting with no shield or arcing sabre, here's **Gracchus**;
He gives thumbs down to that sort of gear—look, it's a trident he
  wields.   202a+203b
And once his right hand has whirred the net he dangles high,
And let it all go, in vain, his bare face showing to the
  spectators   205
Is raised up to them, as he runs for it, all over the arena, so all
  spot who he is.
Let's trust his tunic, when from his throat the gold is
Streaming and bobbing in the ribbon of his tall priest's cap.
Accordingly, it was a humiliation harder to endure than any
Wound for the one told to fight against Gracchus as 'pursuer'.   210

If a free vote were given the People, who would be so

Dead and gone as to hesitate to prefer **Seneca** to **Nero**—
For whose execution there ought to have been kept ready not just
    one
Ape, not just one snake, and not just one sack?
A match for Agamemnon's son was the crime, but the
    circumstances made the case   215
Quite different. The latter in fact acted by authority of the gods,
    to avenge
The slaughter of his father in the middle of the drinks. But he
    never
Stained himself with Electra's jugular, with his Spartan
Spouse's blood; poison for none of his relatives
He brewed; and not once did he sing on stage, as *Orestes*,   220
Or write the *Trojan Wars*. So: what should **Verginius** and his
    armies
Have taken more vengeance for, or else **Galba** in alliance with
    Vindex,
Of all the things **Nero** did in his tyrannical reign, so sadistic, so
    raw?
These are the deeds and these the talents of the blue-blooded
    Emperor,
Who loved foul singing presented to foreigners' stages   225
As his way of soliciting, loved to merit the parsley that crowns a
    Greek.
Let your ancestors' images get the trophies won by your voice:
Before the feet of **Domitius**, go and lay the length of Thyestes'
Train, or Antigone's, or the mask of Melanippe,
Hang up your lyre on your statuesque marble giant.   230

Hey, **Catiline**, take your birth, and **Cethegus**'—
Will anyone find anything higher? Yet your men
Plot armed rising after dark, and arson for our homes and
    temples,
Like boys who belong to the Trouser tribes, descendants of
    Senones,

Daring something that would be O.K. to punish with the *dress of*
    pain. 235
But the consul is awake, confining your units,
And *he* is a man with no past, from Arpinum, no noble,—in fact
    at Rome only lately
A small-town hick of equestrian status—he's stuck all over the
    place a helmeted
picket for everyone panic-stricken, working away on each and
    every hill.
So it was that inside the city-walls his toga brought him as
    much 240
Fame and honorific labelling as at Leucas, as much as,
On Thessaly's plains, **Octavius** stole with his wet
Sword dripping from non-stop slaughter. And, at that, Rome
    called *him* 'Sire',
Rome called **Cicero** the 'Father of the Fatherland', when Rome
    was free.
Up on the Volscians' hill, the other man from Arpinum used 245
To ask for casual work, tiring over a plough owned by someone
    else:
Later on, he would break his knotty vine-staff on anyone's head,
If they were too slow fortifying camp and their pickaxe didn't
    jump to.
Yet he it was that took the Cimbri, the most extreme world-crisis,
Took them on and by himself shielded panicking Rome, 250
And that is the reason why, after there flew off to the Cimbri
    carnage
Crows that had never got near tasting vaster corpses,
His high-born colleague got decorated with laurel in second place.
The souls of the **Decii** were plebeian, plebeian was their
Name: still, in return for all the legions, and for 255
The whole of the auxiliaries and the whole youth of Latium,
They satisfied the underworld gods and mother Earth. 257
A girl-slave's son earned the royal robe and tiara of Quirinus 259
And earned the *fasces*, and *he* was the last of the good kings. 260

The bolts of the gates were betrayed to the tyrants: loosening
    them
For the exiled kings were the young sons of the serving consul,
    whom
A great blow of some description would befit, struck for freedom
    still in doubt,
Something for **Mucius** plus **Cocles** to admire, and the
Girl that swam the boundary of the Roman Empire—River
    Tiber.   265
The hushed-up crimes were disclosed to the Father Senators by a
    slave
Who deserved mourning by Rome's matrons. For those boys, a
    scourging's fair'n'square
Punishment was handed out—the axe first fell by due process of
    law.

I prefer you to have Thersites for father, so long as you are
Like Aeacus' child and take up arms from Vulcan,   270
Rather than for Achilles to beget you, and you be like Thersites.
And yet, however far you reach back, however far you read back
Your name, you derive your clan from the infamy of men who
    took sanctuary:
The first, whoever he was, of your ancestors
Was either a herdsman, or else he was—that
        thing
         I
           refuse
          to
              mention.   275

CHAPTER SIXTEEN

OFF YOU GO AND MAKE A NAME FOR YOURSELF: vv. 39–275

The rest of the poem will continue to traipse back and forth through the imagery of *imagines*, juxtaposing the stuffed-shirt clutter of the Roman kudos factory with other mimetic registers. Thus the marquis is likened to the likeness of a castrated Herm: 'it has a marble head, where *he* is so lifelike an *imago* you would suppose him alive' (vv. 53–5). We meet the inscription of *tituli* (v. 69, 'titles'). Domestic architecture's colonnades are metaphorized (v. 77). Fictional prehistoric extensions of *genus* and *maiores* roam back to mythic absurdity (vv. 131–3, 'descent and ancestors').[146] Ancestors' noble birth 'stands' against the degenerate, 'holds before' them the torch of exposure (vv. 138f., *praeferre*). Grandfather's temple-dedication and *pater*'s triumphal statue come our way (vv. 143f.). We visit the clan-tomb's roadside memorial (v. 146), and witness the award of the *nominis-ac-tituli* of *pater patriae*, that ultimate put-down for aristocracy (vv. 241–4, 'the name-*cum*-title of Father of the Fatherland'). Joining the rest of the lumber, there is the world's *domus*, emptied of its Hellenic master-pieces: paintings, statues, 'ivory touched with life'; and Rome's (so-called) allies, stripped of their household gods, of any artwork worth a second look—all taken as spoils to Rome (vv. 100–10). In the decadent city, those *maiorum effigies* are decked with a singer's *insignia*, tragic costume or an actor's mask; a lyre dangles from a marble colossus (vv. 227–30). But, as this inventory has made clear, the trajectory of the poem has the range to widen out to encompass the globe, as well as back through the centuries.

Juvenal first shoots a speeded-up cartoon version of the career of the élite male. He has the baby born: no credit for choosing your mother (vv. 40–3, cf. v. 14). The lordling steps out, but doesn't wait for salutation, he gets in first with scorn for the mob (vv. 44–6 *vs.* vv. 26–8, esp. *patriam*, v. 45 ~ *patriae*, v. 28). In return, we make a hollow wish for as 'long' a happy life as the genealogy (vv. 46f., *longa*, cf. *longo / sanguine*, vv. 1f.), and remark that an ordinary citizen can be just as special, singular and unique an individual as any bigwig (*Quiritem*, v. 47 ~ *procerem*, v. 26)—and have a greater gift of the gab than his lordship just showed (v. 48). One of *them* can be the law's best champion (vv. 49f. *vs.* v. 25), can show gumption, for a *iuuenis* (youth), and set off across the Empire to bear Roman arms (vv. 51f.).

Think of the addressee as himself a *iuvenem* (v. 71), like (if *un*like) friend Ponticus (vv. 74–6: in the Latin, the wording and concepts pick up the proem, as *futurae / laudis. . . ; sed te censeri laude tuorum / Pontice, noluerim sic ut. . . / esto*, vv. 74f., 79 repeats/rebuts *Pontice, . . . censeri*, vv. 1f., *tuorum /*, v. 22, *metues ne tu sic*, v. 38, *esto /*, v. 21). The addressee is now given a blue-print: from 'be a good soldier', to 'be upright in court if it costs your life' (vv. 79–84). And this is the cue to fast forward the career on out to an 'expectant' world: a spell of provincial administration comes next (vv. 87– 139: he now has a wife, naturally, v. 128). As we just noticed, this *could* ape the worst excesses of Roman looting: a **Dolabella**, an **Antonius**, or **Verres**, bringing back their artwork swag, allied heirlooms, **Marius** 'debagging Africa' (vv. 105–10, 120).[147] Variously righteous-to-cynically corrupt tips bring our hero back home. Let him exaggerate his pedigree as far as he pleases—if he's kept his entourage clean; but if he loses his head, crazed with power somewhere along the way, his forefather's *nobilitas* weighs against him (vv. 127–33, 135–9 *vs.* vv. 88–92). Returned from the tour of duty and in the public eye, his 'failings' carry a high tariff (*animi uitium*, v. 140 negates the proem's *animi bona*, v. 24): a touch of forgery is bound to have him *rendez-vous* in grand-dad's very own temple—before the very eyes of father's triumphal statue (vv. 142–4). Try to hide from the glare of publicity, will you, by moonlighting with somebody's wife, 'wrapped in your riding hood' (vv. 144f.)?

This last picture brings the potted bio-script to its peak, in the poem's overall centre-piece, as bridge to the extended *exemplum* of fatty **Lateranus** the racing *consul* (vv. 146–82): while he is in office, he keeps his drives out of Rome to the hours of darkness, but he'll 'come out' afterwards (vv. 149–54). Did 'we do that too when we were *iuuenes*'? If so, 'go easy on boys, but see it stops with the first shave' (vv. 163–7). **Lateranus**, though, is no babe: *maturus bello* ('seasoned in war'), he belongs on the Empire borders, holding the line as Caesar's *legatus*, not hanging out in the red light district of shame (vv. 169–82). Ponticuses should find this behaviour disgusting in their class (everyone else does), but Juvenal has lots more, ever fouler, *exempla* to spin. . . (vv. 179, 183f.).

Just at this point, this *cursus* has been sarcastically set against 'the standards to be expected of Rome's famous old names': *Volesos Brutumque decebunt. . .* (v. 182). The second half of the poem will set itself to trace scenes from the history of the Roman élite. Back from the recent *cause célèbre* of Domitianic T. Sextius Lateranus (*cos.* 94CE),[148] through the Neronian scenes of nobles on stage and in the arena (vv. 185–210), and that megastar Emperor **Nero** himself (vv. 211–30), to reach the Catilinarian conspirators of the Late Republic, and, via **Cicero** and **Marius**, the ultimate glory days of the Early Republic (vv. 231–57).

Here at the end of the line, before the fall, we meet King Servius Tullius, 'last of the good kings' (vv. 259–60). But the roll-call re-runs a little from there, through the first operations of Justice in the Roman Republic: here, we find that *iuuenes ipsius consulis* ('young sons of the actual consul') are traitors exposed by a slave. These are, precisely, the first Brutus' sons, the first consul's sons, and they have the *fasces* used to sever their necks, rather than adorn their *atrium* and, in time, process ahead for their funeral trains (vv. 261–8).

Juvenal's historical survey of Roman *exempla* for his trainee hero shows only non-nobles and plebs doing their duty. His *envoi* underlines that the conception he has pursued to flesh out his advertised ideal of *uirtus* (a term which, symptomatically, never re-appears in his text after v. 20; *nobilitas* recurs at v. 139) is the most traditional Roman construal, to all appearances untrammelled by any philosophical subtlety. Juvenal's strictures would fashion an epic hero:

* 'A Virgilian *alius Achilles* or, to be plain, a worthy son for Homer's Achilles' (vv. 269f.)[149]

Which is to say, Juvenal licks into shape his own hallowed *warrior* for fresh *arma uirumque* ('Arms and the Man', the first words and project of Virgil's *Aeneid*). Approaching *uirtus* through the portals of the aristocratic *domus* has conditioned and pre-cast the conceptualization of human excellence open to view. The exhibition of armour in this hall of manhood-mirrors is for us to idolize or trash, without challenge from any other image-repertoire. Satire pretends it would like to extol a military success worthy of its epic hexameters.

Thus Juvenal pushed his Ponticus off to the army (v. 69), to run a province (vv. 87–139). He wanted **Lateranus** off to the Eastern or Northern fronts (vv. 169f.). His Neronian *Fabii* and *Mamerci* tread the boards rather than turn swords on themselves (vv. 191–5). **Gracchus** in the arena does his fighting, but not *in armis*, as a Gaul with a shield, even a scimitar, but rather plays run-away with net and spear, his 'face' shown off to the crowd (vv. 200–10: *uoltum /*, 205. Cf. *uoltus /*, 2; *agnoscendus*, 206, cf. *agnosco*, 26). **Nero** played parricide assassin Orestes on stage: **Verginius** Rufus, **Galba** and **Vindex** (The Avenger) had to use their *armis* for *this* miserable revenge (vv. 211–30: 221f.). The Catilinarians aimed their *arma* at Rome, like (true) descendants of the Gauls who sacked the city: they deserved to become Neronian human torches, like the Christians punished for torching Rome (vv. 231–5). But **Cicero** put guards in helmets everywhere and climbed all seven *montes* ('hills') to zap them (vv. 237–40). The young **Octavius** had to leave Rome and 'butcher with dripping sword' from Actium all the way (back) to Philippi, to win as much fame for his name, *if* he ever did. . . (Octavius, i. e. Augustus in boyhood, vv. 241–4).

Marius went through Juvenal's recommended programme: in the ranks, then sole saviour of Rome from the giant Cimbri invaders (vv. 245–53). Finally, the **Decii** once spelled 'plebs', but now they are *nomina*, 'the name of fame'. 'Worth whole legions, allied squadrons, and every single young man in Latium', as they jumped to Hell (vv. 254–7. Note *pube*. . . ['youth'], 256). And that 'last good king' was 'a slave-girl's son, but earned tiara and fasces' (vv. 259f., *natus*, 259. Cf. *natus*, v. 14, *fascis*, v. 260, cf. *uirgas*, v. 23), whereas the first consul's sons had the *fasces* turned on them. . .

As the satirist's story of Rome depressively disrecommends Empire *and* Republic, mocks nostalgia in epic and historical roll-calls alike, he winds up bidding us *Pontici* to take up *arma* like Achilles, whoever our fathers may be. We are all alike, Neros not just bound by our fathers to kill, but programmed to sing the song which binds us to killing for our fathers, and to play our ephebe son's part to the hilt. For the *fasces* that ushered the Roman aristocrat into their Hall of Fame symbolised the sovereignty that went back through the Brutuses and Servius Tullius, to *Quirinus* (v. 259). And before *Quirinus* changed his name, and ceased to be known as Romulus, he gathered Rome's founding fathers together in the first place by declaring an asylum for the undesirables of everywhere (vv. 269–75).

Juvenal's tour of Roman history noticed a string of names never to be included in any roll-call of Roman fame: the appearance of *Volesos Brutumque* (v. 182)[150] underlines how far the non-entity villains **Capito** and **Tutor** (v. 93), **Pansa** and **Natta** (v. 96), the infamous looters **Dolabella**, **Antonius** and **Verres** (v. 105f.), notorious **Marius** (v. 120)[151] and **Lateranus** (v. 147),[152] have taken us from the Republican heroes celebrated in the classics, from Ennius and Livy, from Horace and Virgil.

Returned to Rome, Juvenal's theatre featured the star-name **Lentulus** (v. 187),[153] with **Fabii** and **Mamerci** (vv. 191f.),[154] then a noble **Gracchus** in the arena (vv. 201–10);[155] a late **Galba**, with **Verginius** and **Vindex** (vv. 221f.), must put the nadir Julio-Claudian **Nero** down, last of the Claudii Nerones and, he had made quite sure, last of the Domitii Ahenobarbi, too (vv. 193, 212–23).[156] But in Cicero's **Catiline** and **Cethegus** we meet canonical sinners of Rome (vv. 231–5);[157] before

Marius (vv. 245–53),[158] the **Decii** (vv. 254–7)[159] and King Servius Tullius (vv. 259–60)[160] haul us back to the core of epic catabasis and historical exemplarity, and back to the poetic canon.

Finally and conclusively, under the deploring gaze of heroic **Mucius** Scaevola, Horatius **Cocles** and Cloelia (vv. 264f.),[161] Juvenal executes the sons of Brutus (vv. 261–8) who stoop straight out of *Aeneid* 6.[162]

Juvenal's Roman roll-call is not just back-to-front; he has put down the Julio-Claudians, from **Octavius'** butchery to **Nero's** elimination, then looked for Late Republican *uirtus* and found it only in Octavian's father-figure and martyr-victim **Cicero's** intramural suppression of perverted aristocratic *arma*. His real soldier-brute **Marius** behaved just *exactly* the way Juvenal demands Ponticus should *not* handle his provincial command (*nodosam. . . frangebat uertice uitem* ['he would break his knotty vine-staff on heads'], v. 247 ~ *si frangis uirgas sociorum in sanguine* ['if you break canes in the blood of allied troops'], v. 136); but if **Marius'** triumph celebrates undimmed salvation of Rome, nevertheless it is ingloriously defensive action, warding off barbarian invasion. It is not Roman imperial conquest, which is entirely erased from the picture as Juvenal skips over the Scipiones–Fabii–Aemilii names for fame entirely and leaps back past them to the **Decii**. The glory days (of Ennius' life and texts) are kept out of sight, in the closet.

Moreover, and worse still, the suicidal heroism of the *Decii* retroactively reminds the reader to continue, and finish, **Marius'** story. Just as notice of Augustus finished **Cicero's** (and mention of Cicero finished the Catilinarians', and **Galba** & co. finished **Nero's** stories). For plural *Decii* partner *Marii* plural in Roman poetic roll-calls to introduce the shadow of Marius' terroristic finale and his (adoptive) son, whose failure against Sulla forced his suicide as the premature consul of 82, with only orders for a massacre in Rome to his name. *Decii*, as Juvenal caustically underlines by having them devote themselves to 'parent' Earth (v. 257), spell dynastic cloning *par exemple*: the father P. Decius Mus, as the family's first consul, sacrificed himself against the Latins in 340; the son P. Decius Mus followed suit as *cos. IV* in 295 against the Samnites; and, in Cicero's book, at least, the grandson P. Decius Mus carbon-copied, as *cos.* in 279 against Pyrrhus.[163]

The family tradition of the **Decii** required them to have sons to throw them away for Rome, yet preserve enough to supply further generations of the clan. With them, Satire's flopped-epic version of How the West was Won is done, for we reach straight to the Age of Kings, where we head straight for Servius Tullius, the king smeared as slave-born, the cuckoo in Tarquinius Priscus' nest who ousted Tarquin's sons, when Tarquin's predecessor Ancus Martius' sons killed him to stop the diadem of Romulus decorating a servile cranium. In the end, Tarquin's son (or grandson) Superbus would claim his birthright and have his father-in-law Tullius cut down to size.[164]

Meantime, 'The Conquest of Italy' has folded away into Decian 'dittoes', and only the resistance to Porsenna, **Mucius**, **Cocles** and Cloelia, attests The Liberation from the Tyrants. All these appear, however, only as back-grounded spectators at the scenario of disgrace brought by Sons on the house of Brutus. Juvenal's 'hero' is someone quite other. He is the slave (Vindicius) who exposed the treachery of the first consul's sons. He is the one who deserves the funeral honours awarded to Brutus, founder of the Roman Republic, remembered here as but the father of scum.[165]

To reach this denouement of *Annales manqués*, we must negotiate the utterant's high modality throughout our performance of his script. Speaking out against aristocratic *folies de grandeur* has made him a rave from the Republican grave. He has spoken up vigorously in the name of a sovereign 'us', whose say-so 'bestows praise on winners in our circus' (vv. 58f., *laudamus. . . facili. . . palma. . . et rauco. . . circo*).[166] 'We are the ones who hand out honours, now as always' (*damus et dedimus*, v. 70).

Juvenal has urged the good prospect to resist and die rather than to submit to any Emperor Tyrant's orders to lie (vv. 81–4), even if he did then despair of retribution for the corrupt (v. 97). His **Lateranus'** speak-easy is full of a levelling down he can ironically dub *aequa. . . libertas* (*liberté, égalité*, v. 177), and he flays the *populus* for playing along with **Nero's** degradations (vv. 188–90). *Retiarius* ('gladiator armed with the net') **Gracchus** 'shames', not just his opponent, but 'the whole city' (vv. 210, 200, *dedecus urbis*). Really carried away, the speaker must for a second imagine 'a Rome free to vote' on candidates for Emperor: *libera si dentur populo suffragia*. . . (vv. 211f.).

Even if we do shy right away into daft execration of Nero's singing and poetastry above his deathtoll, **Nero** sets the stage for Juvenal to direct a pantomime from history of revenge on the wicked king, in which we are brought to contemplate the dejection of one of Rome's two and a half imperial dynasties up to the time of his writing (vv. 221–3).

And **Cicero** has us lose our cool completely, as the subject of this saviour in a *toga* makes us huff and puff him higher than the insulted *Octauius*, denuded of the new clothes of his title Augustus, and denied Rome's genuine salute: *Roma parentem, / Roma patrem patriae Ciceronem libera dixit* (vv. 243f., 'When Rome dubbed **Cicero** "Parent and Father of the Fatherland", Rome was *free'*). As the divine eponym of all Roman Caesars is set alongside **Cicero**'s Catilinarian conspirators and **Marius'** barbarian Cimbri, we are led to our ultimate primal scene, the *Liberator* father's revenge on his treacherous royalist boys.

The genetic destiny of their noble birth called for great exploits, certainly, but *magnum aliquid dubia pro libertate* (v. 263, 'Something heroic for freedom in jeopardy'). Not only in the chancy first days of the *res publica libera* was—is—*libertas dubia* ('freedom in doubt', v. 263). Nor only when fathers hand on to sons.

• '*Satire*'s liberties are, by right, in permanent jeopardy.'

The speaker's profile proposes a declaimer transported by his theme back through the centuries. He makes sure we see he *knows* he's (only) performing, though, when he pauses to admire a particularly striking verbal felicity, by asseverating it is no such thing, but rather oracular truth:

• '*quod modo proposui, non est sententia, uerum est. / credite me uobis folium recitare Sibyllae.*' (vv. 125f.)

What I just stated is no *dictum*, it's true; trust me, I'm reciting to you the Book of Revelations.

This is a 'recitation', precisely, which proclaims that it turns the screw of ever more salacious depths of depravity as the reader wades on, wallowing in worse (i. e. better) *exempla* (vv. 183f.). For all that he takes us to the theatre of depravity, pretending to wish a 'real crucifixion' on the actor (*uera cruce*, v. 188), Juvenal's game is to wander in and out of the declamation hall where he roars, in and out of the history of praise and censure at Rome.

All along he made it clear that his target was to brutalize the Roman Son, figured as Ponticus. To use that assault to play with Roman myth, its iconology and hagiography. He disclaims any seditious project, as traditionally Catonian as any second-century Hadrianic subject could get. He positions the present as a decayed cultural isotope, the past as active waste-pile. But at the same time, he takes his disavowal to pieces, and shoves them our way, to cope with however we may imagine a 'free public' might. As if the very possibility of genuine reflection belongs back in a reality closed off for ever generations before. 'Political thought is a dodo' is itself a forceful piece of political thinking, for all its dystopian despair.

For when Ponticus' proem closed, Juvenal at once retroactively cancelled the address, declaring that its rough invective had been aimed at another (*monui* ['I admonished'], v. 39). He set up a 'historical name', of a sort, to play deplorable dead foil to Ponticus (*quem. . . fama. . ., tradit*, vv. 71f.), heaped a re-play of brutal scorn on him as if it is 'real business' (*tecum mihi sermo. . .* ['my discussion is with you'], v. 39), before turning back to his cap, Ponticus, for a string of more or less positive paternal precepts.[167]

As we guess, the same decline in tone that Juvenal showed off in the proem (vv. 21–38) sets in again, so that by the time Ponticus is brought back from service abroad to Rome, he is insulted as a sacrilegious forger and hooded would-be nocturnal sex-prowler (vv. 142–5)!

Juvenal's charade with his dummy-speaker is laid before the reader as just a prime tactic to beat the censor and lambast just such a young bud as Ponticus. That must be why he chose out the dubious valency of the speaking name **Rubelli / Blande** for his mutt (vv. 39f.). Rubellius Blandus *(cos. suff.* 18CE), whose marriage to Tiberius' granddaughter, Drusus Caesar's daughter, Julia in 33CE is deplored by the historian, was grandson of an *eques* from Tibur.[168] We know two sons: Rubellius Plautus, 'through his mother's origin, his degree of descent from St Augustus was on a par with Nero's', was accompanied into exile in 60CE by his wife Antistia, but would still lose his head in 62CE—before his posthumous deletion from the senate, 'a joke worse than its sin': '*nobilitas* through his mother, from the Julian family' made and broke his name;[169] and Rubellius Drusus.[170] So posit a third brother, pigling *Blandus*, decide Juvenal is in error, or doesn't care for historical accuracy, or wants to make quite sure his **Rubellius Blandus** stays in the world of fantasy (cf. *fama*, v. 71). Or recall that the offending (great)grandfather in Tibur had been 'a famous teacher of rhetoric'.[171] Then see that the poet 'likes' *Rubellius Blandus* for the name: it spells upward mobility through the 'eloquence' business (cf. *Quiritem / facundum*, vv. 48f.). And it *says* 'Blushkin' (< *rubellus*, 'Rubens' red'), 'The Sweet-Talker' (*blandus*). Above all, it *does* the game of the *cognomen*, at once naming famous 'charm' and 'compliment', and defaming notorious 'seduction' and 'adulation'.

As such, *Rubellius Blandus* is a 'rhetorical figure' whose role is to suffer what he bespeaks. Juvenal *shames* him with rough talk, as a channel for *winsome persuasion* of Ponticus. *Blandus* reminds us that *Ponticus* itself may all along *say* 'scion of a triumphal hero of Roman conquest' but *mean* 'barbarian slave-import, off the latest boat'. As Juvenal o-so-rudely pointed out 'to **Blandus**', what we mean when we use even the most heraldic of names—'*Creticus* or *Camerinus*'—all depends who speaks, which 'we'.

The essential *point* of the deliberately exposed manoeuvre with *Blandus*, however, is to show, but not *say*, that *Ponticus* is all along to be a strategy, no more nor less, through which to *point* at *us*.

CHAPTER SEVENTEEN

ON YOUR WAY OUT, IF YOU WOULDN'T MIND. . . : JUVENAL, *SATIRES, BOOK 3*

- 'So long as there are patriarchs there will be Ponticuses.'

  For moralists to bully.

  For satirists to knock out their stuffing.

The Roman *iuuenis* was lectured, each time he crossed his family's threshold, that he carried the fame of his name wherever he would go. The ancestral *imagines* preached 'respect' (*maiorum respectus, gratia. . . / umbrarum,* vv. 64f. ; cf. *respice quod moneant leges. . .,* ['respect what the laws preach'], v. 91). Which is to say, the gaze back into the past *was* that basic lesson in prestige, the pile-driving imperative from the stacked *atrium* that brought the poem momentum and trajectory, sufficient to sustain its drive to dominate its audience.

- *Stemmata quid faciunt?*

is even presented by Juvenal's *volume* as a version of the Roman educational system at work inculcating national and dynastic taxidermy into the next generation of fiefs.

The book's opening poem *Satire* 7 has just used acclamation of an imperial injection of patronage into 'the arts' to kick-start, review and so rip to shreds the whole montage of institutional apparatus geared into the production of Roman *kultchur* (vv. 1–36).[172] Poets (vv. 36–97) yield to historians (vv. 98–104), and we zip through Law (vv. 105–49), to slide eventually down to teaching in class. The *rhetores* 'teach declamation', to young *Achilleses*, to their *iuuentus* (youth, vv. 150–214: 210, 213). At the bottom of the pile, the *grammaticus* faces a roomful of *pueri* (boys), with his faded Horace and begrimed Virgil (vv. 215–43: 226f., cf. 62, 69). He must read the histories, know the entire canon better than his own hands, so he can answer any dumb question about the set texts (vv. 230–6). The patriarchs demand that he 'mould their unformed *mores* like a sculptor' (*ut si quis cera uoltum facit*, vv. 237f.).

And this is *precisely* what Juvenal will try his thumb at next, giving every Ponticus among his naughty class of *tot puerorum* ('all those boys', v. 240) a stinging but subtly camouflaged dressing-down, replete with *his* homework on the Classics. Through every line of

• *Stemmata quid faciunt?*

we could (should) be thinking of the performance as a loving caricature of this very Mr Chips.

A whole supporting series of triggers signals complicity between the two compositions: both poems emphatically repudiate bearing false witness (7. 13–16 ~ vv. 80–4). Both orient to young men (*o iuuenes*, 7. 20). Poets foolishly 'bother with the same genteel': *tu Camerinos / at Baream, tu nobilium magna atria curas?* (7. 90f. ~ *Camerinus /*, v. 38). *Fabius* and *Lentulus* are cited as patrons of old (7. 95 ~ vv. 187, 191). Both the practising lawyer stands to declaim *dubia pro libertate*, and Brutus' sons should have pitched for greatness *dubia pro libertate* (7. 116 ~ v. 263). 'What price eloquence?' re-echoes in Nero's 'insignia of eloquence' (*quod uocis pretium?*, 7. 119 ~ *insignia uocis*, v. 227). Advocate **Aemilius** will be paid in full, because he has a bronze 'chariot' in his porch, and an 'equestrian statue' of himself, dashing to war (*currus, sedens, statua*, 7. 124–8 ~ *stantis in curribus Aemilianos*, v. 3). Thoughts of **Cicero** (7. 139 ~ vv. 237–44) precede the interminable declamation pegged to Hannibal after Cannae (7. 161–4 ~ Fabius, v.

14), and the topic is *facundia* ('eloquence', 7. 145 ~ v. 48). The millionaire's dining-suite rises on tall columns, such as the noble's house rests upon (7. 182f. ~ v. 77). First *rhetor* to *consul* or *consul* to *rhetor*, then Lateranus the *mulio consul* (7. 197f. ~ v. 148). Think of the rise of Servius *Tullius*, last of the good kings (7. 199f. ~ vv. 259f.). Class nicknames teacher '*Allobrog* Cicero' (7. 214 ~ *Allobrogicis*, v. 13). All this before that final clinching imagery of the teacher as 'sculptor-*cum-imago* artist' (7. 238 ~ *uultus*, v. 2, *cerae*, v. 19).

Dovetailing the two performances together will re-double the burden of malevolence which the poem slips onto its audience. For these pupils were daddy's boys, who *will* be boys, lined up at the back of Juvenal's classroom, doing the dirty, habit-forming, things that everyone knows, but nobody talks, about (vv. 239–41).

When Juvenal's lecture on *The Pedigree* ends in *its* final aposiopesis, to cover those inexpressibly foul founders of Rome,[173] the teacher's class stop too, as they stop with poem 7, 'eyes trembling at' such a remarkable 'climax' (7. 241, *oculos. . . in fine trementis*).

And when their (our) eyes open again, there 'heaves into sight', out cruising the streets of Rome, larger than life (*occurras*, v. 2), Juvenal's finest creation, the contemporary but inexpressibly foul creature Naevolus, the lusciously male self-prostituting hero of poem 9. Remember the *imagines*, when he tells us of his career servicing the *patres*, disposing of *mater*'s virginity, and fathering the whole brood of children (9. 26, 43–6; 72; 74–90). This 'ass on two legs' is himself a master-image, the disfigurement of *uirtus Romana*.[174]

It is not, perhaps, a surprise that the book's final image will be of a new Odysseus' ears stopped with wax to elude Siren song, the last word 'deaf' (. . . *surdo*, 9. 150). If, that is, you're listening,

• '—Err. Sorry. Could you repeat the question, please? —',

if you're still there, FIGURING OUT ROMAN NOBILITY, and not, figuratively, caught—

IN FINE

APPENDIX 1

HORACE, *ODES* 1. 12 AND THE 'GENERALIZING PLURAL': DISCUSSION (WITH TEXT AND TRANSLATION)

Horace, *Odes* 1. 12 is far from providing an uncontroversial paradigm for the rhetorical figuration of exemplary names for fame. Rather, the argument will run, this canonical lyric is from first to last precisely an *exploration* of the problematic of the specificity of praise.

1 TEXT

Quem uirum aut heroa lyra uel acri
tibia sumis celebrare, Clio?
quem deum? cuius recinet iocosa
  nomen imago

aut in umbrosis Heliconis oris 5
aut super Pindo gelidoue in Haemo,
unde uocalem temere insecutae
  Orphea siluae

arte materna rapidos morantem
fluminum lapsus celerisque uentos,   10
blandum et auritas fidibus canoris
     ducere quercus?

quid prius dicam solitis parentis
laudibus, qui res hominum et deorum,
qui mare et terras uariisque mundum   15
     temperat horis?

unde nil maius generatur ipso,
nec uiget quicquam simile aut secundum:
proximos illi tamen occupauit
     Pallas honores.   20

proeliis audax, neque te silebo,
Liber, et saeuis inimica Virgo
beluis, nec te, metuende certa
     Phoebe sagitta.

dicam et Alciden puerosque Ledae,   25
hunc equis, illum superare pugnis
nobilem; quorum simul alba nautis
     stella refulsit,

defluit saxis agitatus umor,
concidunt uenti fugiuntque nubes,   30
et minax, quod sic uoluere, ponto
     unda recumbit.

Romulum post hos prius an quietum
Pompili regnum memorem an superbos
Tarquini fascis, dubito, an **Catonis**   35
     nobile letum.

98

Regulum et Scauros animaeque magnae
prodigum Paulum superante Poeno
gratus insigni referam Camena
    Fabriciumque.   40

hunc et incomptis Curium capillis
utilem bello tulit et Camillum
saeua paupertas et auitus apto
    cum lare fundus.

crescit occulto uelut arbor aeuo   45
fama Marcelli; micat inter omnis
Iulium sidus uelut inter ignis
    luna minores.

gentis humanae pater atque custos,
orte Saturno, tibi cura magni   50
Caesaris fatis data: tu secundo
    Caesare regnes.

ille seu Parthos Latio imminentis
egerit iusto domitos triumpho,
siue subiectos Orientis orae   55
    Seras et Indos,

te minor laetum reget aequus orbem;
tu graui curru quaties Olympum,
tu parum castis inimica mittes
    fulmina lucis.   60

2 TRANSLATION

Who is the hero or demigod that on lyre or treble
Aulos you're set to celebrate, Clio my Muse?
Who is the god? Who will the playful after-image
    Re-echo by name,

Either in the shadowed bounds of Helicon   5
Or up on Pindus, maybe in the chill of Haemus,
From where, at his melodious song, there homed pell-mell
    On Orpheus whole forests,

As, with skill owed his mother, he braked surging
River currents and gusting winds,   10
While his charm used lyrical chords on the ears
    Of oaks, for his train.

What should I say ahead of the traditional praises
Of the father, who hath the realms of humans and gods,
Ocean and continents, the cosmos, in all its changing
    Round of seasons blended?   15

From him is conceived nothing greater than himself,
Nor is any living thing his like, or anywhere close behind:
The next place to him, though, was taken for her own by
    Pallas, in the scale of honours.   20

Cavalier in battle, I shan't muffle either of you,
Liber and the Maiden who persecutes savage
Beasts, nor you, a terror with your unerring
    Arrows, Phoebus Apollo.

I shall tell of you, too, Hercules grandson of Alcaeus, and Leda's
    boys,   25
One on horse, the other with fists, both winners
And nobly so; the instant the sailors see their bright
    Star's dazzle,

Down from the rocks runs the churning water,
Calm drop the winds and away scatter storm-clouds;   30
And for all their menace, because this is their will, across the sea
    The waves settle.

Romulus after all these first, or the tranquil
Numa's reign, which should I recount, or the haughty
Tarquin's *fasces*—I'm just not sure—or **Cato's**   *35*
   Noble death?

Regulus and the **Scauri**, the mighty soul, too,
That **Paulus** threw away when Carthage was on top
I'll relate, in thanks, with distinction from my Muse
   — Along with **Fabricius**.   *40*

This last, and **Curius** whose hair was kept unkempt,
Was produced to be useful in war, as also **Camillus**,
By savage deprivation and, from their forefathers, to match,
   By a farm with its household spirit.

Growing just as a tree grows behind the veil of time passing   *45*
Is the fame of **Marcellus**; in the company of all the rest sparks
The **Julian** constellation, just as in its company of flares
   The moon dwarfs the rest.

Father and protector of the human race,
Offspring of Saturn, to you nurture of great   *50*
Caesar has been entrusted by destiny: you, and, always right
   behind you,
   Caesar next in line, must rule your realm.

He, it might be the Parthians who loom over Latium
That he drives into subjection with a triumph fair and square,
Or upon the reduction of far-Eastern shores,   *55*
   The peoples of China and India,

Will rule a world of joy, righteous in subordination to you;
You and your massive chariot will rattle Olympus,
You will launch in persecution of depraved
   Holy clearings your arsenal of thunderbolts.   *60*

3 DISCUSSION

Different echoes play tricks on the Muse/Poem, *Clio* (*Cleo* < *Kleiô*?), herself an echo of *celebrare* (v. 2), Horace by another name. Indeed the words already enact this in the doubling audible in this enunciation. Clio's intonation of an honoured name, 'a man or hero', depends on which instrument(s) play the song, in what locale, and before the ears of what audience (vv. 1–12). The oaks in Horace's wood model the poet's audience: the infidel groves that earn Jove's wrath (vv. 59f.) are the exorcized 'you's' who play deaf to the hymn's complaisant pieties; these profane sinners, banished from the congregation, must face the solidary team of propitiators and propitiated. Love Horace; or hate Heaven and its deputy on Earth, and expect to be hated by all.[175]

So Clio draws on all the praises in the repertoire to fashion this hymn, re-deploying specific names chosen from the stock, thereby invoking specific fame (and its stories), to make a special song of songs. *Every* playful sound represents a power-play in the propitiation of unutterable Power. *All* of it is 'imagery', word-echoes of name-fame, verbal re-verb.

Clio knows the rule that praise should start from the inimitable Almighty father, the cosmic Emperor. In the impossibly risky second place, audacious as ever, comes his daughter *Pallas* the generalissimo; Clio will risk taking the liberty of naming, so praising, *Liber* next, thus vindicating his filiation (vv. 13–22). Perhaps Clio is the audacious one (*audax*, v. 21), sticking *her* neck out by letting the phrase 'daring in battle' oscillate between Athena and Bacchus (*Pallas* and *Liber*), or else echo on from one item into the next. Next we recognize in *Virgo* and *Phoebus* Leto's twins (vv. 22–5): we could just as well dub them *Phoebe* (Diana) and *Apollo*. *Alcides* (v. 25) is the 'adoptive' son of Amphitryon, fathered by Jove on Alcmena and (some say) named for Amphitryon's father Alcaeus; and finally, when 'Leda's boys' are differentiated by their sphere of excellence (*nobilem*), we recognize (in both senses of the word) the *Dioskouroi* ('Zeus' lads' in Greek), in playful matronymic guise (vv. 25–7).

Praising all these gods shows that to praise them is to praise the dynasty of their common father, one universal family on a *stemma*, a regime that brings peace (vv. 22–32). Both sets of twins present 'teamwork', slaughterous (of beasts), then eirenic. With Liber and Hercules, we find contested paternity raising to Olympus sons who made good; Castor and Pollux, we know, pool divinity *between* them; they straddle the divine/mortal boundary.

This material is, however, to serve as rhetorical foil cueing the 'real' focus of the Roman song of praise to follow, which will swell, throughout, the praises of Saturn's son Jove, father of the whole human *gens*. Thus the founder Romulus takes up from the (Graeco-Roman) 'gods', because (as *Quirinus*) he ascended to join his grandfather Jove, alongside Hercules and the Gemini (v. 33).

Next, the poet's tentative plunge into Roman history (vv. 33–5) makes the roll-call of *nomina* that follows (vv. 33–46) half-detach itself from what precedes, to form up eventually as the entourage of 'lesser lights shining round the Julian star' (vv. 46–8). We sing into affirmation the right of Augustus' Iulii to a pseudo-dynastic pre-eminence over all the *gentes* of Rome; we put the dependants of the line of Iulus back through Aeneas and Anchises-Venus to Jove at the service of the Almighty father, through their representative, his vice-gerent and descendant, *Caesar*, down on planet Earth (vv. 50–2). *He* plays the terrestrial equivalent of bold Field-Marshal Pallas, Jove's second-in-command, and wins peace for the mundane Empire just as the heavenly twins calm storms in nature (vv. 46– 60, cf. 18–20, 27–32).

Praise of each member of the two catalogues has been individually customized. The pecking-order, the claims for priority, are factored into their ordering. The ensembles are *narrativized* (supplied with an implicit narrative) in accordance with their roles in the overarching programme of the poem. And, supremely, the stake of the poem is to offer praise to Augustus by subordinating him to Jove; that is, to articulate and *image* the power of Augustus by analogy with the Almighty's unfettered dynastics, only with the paradigmatic substitution of pious obedience to the authority of the Almighty in the place of domination through direct paternity. In Augustus' triumph, he will represent Jupiter, who need not ride *his* chariot down from the sky (vv.

54, 58). Jupiter will reign over all, but he won't *need* to reign over all, because this *Caesar* is his 'second', he looks 'auspiciously' on Jove's reign, deigns to present no threat, his auspicious name is his fame, 'The August' one (*tu secundo Caesare regnes*, vv. 51f., audaciously shadows a repressed but audible *ille secundo Ioue regnet*, 'let him rule his realm with Jove right behind him and next in line').[176]

Here we are, then, here we hear: one praise, many praises; one praised, many praised; and through every line, pairs of doublets, strings of blurred statuses between heaven and earth, the echoic shadowing of leader and second-in-command, the imagery of the 'original', Jove, used to imagine the power of his 'copy', *Caesar*, and so, too, *vice versa*. It is not hard to see how powerfully the discourse of this hymn to omnipotence in two ontological domains presses its concepts toward a unity in all pluralities, but fission within that unity. It is within the frame of this paean that the catalogue of Roman heroism, with its singulars and its plural, cries out to be reckoned. Horace performs the blurring of statuses that praise inevitably brings in its train, even as it must scrupulously respect and vindicate the exact specifics that individuate the recipients of praise. 'Man, or hero, demigod or god. . .' is the choice that must get/risks getting lost whenever encomium gets under way. Specificity must vie with typicality, singularity with generalization.

The song charms peace, respecting the power of (both) the Cos-mocrat(s) in its dual world, but playfully recording the Muse in a mega-mix of all the traditions of world music. 'On lyre, on pipe', (choral) reeds and (monodic) strings (vv. 1f.), we must sing a bi-, or super-, or supra-, cultural re-envisioning, under the spell of *our* Orphic conductor, Horace. In this poetic echo-chamber of Olympian Pindaric whispers, audible through their jolly Sapphic jingle, *Clio* and *Camena* (vv. 2, 39) duet together, at once devout and naughty, on a medley of cosmocracy through theogony, with political ascendancy through his-torical subordination. Risking fun and making fun of risk as they go. The uplift of devotion is stressed in scholarship; the blithe exultation is not.

Such, in a rush, is the context for pondering our topic here, the specific singularity or the generalizing plural in *Scauros*, which appears in the middle of Horace's catalogue of Romans (v. 37). He has put first things first, with the Founding Father *Romulus* (v. 33), but 'wondered whether' his pacific 'second' Numa doesn't deserve to come 'next' (. . . *prius an. . . memorem an. . . dubito*, vv. 33–5); not that Numa earned consecration, but that he incarnates the pious successor whose calm may be what Rome wants most, from its Jovial Caesar (vv. 33f. : / *Romulum. . . quietum* / : quietus for dead Numa, not a deified *Quirinum* / ?).[177]

There was only one Romulus, but Rome knew more *Pompilii* than meet the eye: all the Calpurnii Pisones, claiming descent from Numa's son Calpus, knew that *Pompilius sanguis* meant them ('Pompilian blood', Hor. *Ars Poet.* 292).

Or, would Clio do better to sing of / *Tarquini*, in place of / *Pompili* (or / *Romulum*, vv. 34–5, 33)? The **Tarquin** *gens* was banished from Rome to bless the Republic: the reference can only be between the two kings, *Priscus*, who introduced the *fasces* to Roman pride (*prius,. . . fasces*, vv. 33–5), or *Superbus*, the 'proud' conqueror (*superbos* / *Tarquini*, vv. 34f.).

Does this mention suggest that the Muse 'would have' explained why her selection to represent Romanness brought additional praise to the Almighty? Does her modal dubitation tell *us* to pause and see what form of 'nobility' we would be promoting if we made one choice rather than another?

Or rather, I find myself wondering, does Clio's wondering prompt us to see in what order in what scale of values. . ., or with what priorities between scales of value. . ., or within what co-ordinates. . ., her praise should operate? And has she not pegged out for us the discursive field for a *contest in* praise?[178]

One possible nominee could be (could it?) the 'noble death of **Cato**' (vv. 35f.)—or indeed any of the run of names in the first two lines of the next stanza, which seems to run on with further suggestions, as they occur to Clio, in an echo-sequence:

/ *Romulum post hos* ~
/ *Regulum et Scauros,*

/ *Pompili regnum* ~
/ *prodigum Paulum,*
. . . *an superbos* / ~
. . . *superante Poeno* / (vv. 33f. ~ vv. 37f.)

Putting Roman 'heroes' second to the gods *is* harder than putting Pallas, or Caesar, second to the Almighty: Clio is bound to 'fail', so that her failure will perform Roman subordination in pious modesty before the Olympians (*prius dicam*, v. 13 *vs. dicam*, v. 25, *prius*, v. 33).

Some Romans served Rome with *their* 'failure': would it be hybristic pride to set success in war above Numa's abstention from *res gestae* (concrete success)? Or *vice versa*? Is decision either way invidious? (Notice that Mars was away from the divine list; but Apollo, at least, was armed, v. 24. . .) Would the story parcelled up in Tarquinius Superbus's name-for-fame tell us rather of his fall into tyranny and overthrow? Does *Tarquin* spell the consecration of Rome as the *respublica libera* (of Livy, *A. U. C.* 2. 1. 1, 'Republican *liberté*')? Didn't the Roman rods of *imperium*, the human scale 'echo' of Jove's *fulmina* (v. 60, 'bolts'), acquire their *superbia* from Tarquin(s), but *legitimate* it through Brutus the Liberator?

Now Horace's praise-poem already pre-echoes Virgil's roll-call in *Aeneid* 6, each text the other's first critique (a synopsis of the scene, 756–886, is given in Appendix 2). Virgil will reach the foundation of the imperium with the words: *his* / *Romulus* at 6. 778. Moving, without Horatian dubitation, straight to *Caesar*, all the Iulii, and *Augustus Caesar* advancing the *imperium* (vv. 789–95), Anchises' praises overshadow *Alcides* (v. 801) and *Liber* (v. 805), before resuming with the (nameless) Numa and (in order of succession) the rest of the kings, from vv. 810–16,[179] and so reaching *Tarquinios reges animamque superbam* / *ultoris Bruti fascisque. . . receptos* (vv. 817f., 'the Tarquin Kings, and the proud soul of Brutus the Avenger, and the vindication of the *fasces*').

Virgil's Tarquins merge into a *non*-generalizing plural, where Horace uses a referentially ambivalent singular.[180] The conversion, through the hinge of the verse-unit, of the regal name's pride into the proud soul of the Republic contrasts with Horace's hinge that links/disjoins his 'pride' (*superbos* /), his Tarquin, his *fasces*. As we have seen before in this study, Anchises is showing how 'sovereignty' is undiminished when the first consul implements *imperium* by turning the lictors' axes on his traitor-sons: so absolute can *amor patriae* become ('love of your country', vv. 819–23).

Virgil's spate of Republican *exempla* comes next (vv. 824f., 836–46), interrupted by the unnamed gladiatorial pair of Pompey and Caesar (vv. 826–35), and then the roll-call is done, but for the supplementary **Marcelli** (vv. 854ff.).

Now (in *his* version of 'dubitation') Anchises signals that his grim portrait of Brutus the Liberator stemmatically foreshadows Brutus the Tyrannicide, who will play a re-mix of father and miscreant sons: did he not die for freedom and love of country, a traitor put down by the legitimate Roman authorities, a Brutus misled by unbounded love of fame, the primal fame in his name? (vv. 821ff. '. . . however [the Liberator's] descendants will view the old story, or stories, of the Bruti. . .' *tells* readers to think over the Tyrannicide's misguided devotion to his family's legacy of 'killing-and-dying for fair Freedom'. A Brutus will execute his nearest and dearest for Rome, even if he deserves to die for it—isn't that the point?).[181]

Horace's pride of Tarquin(s) contains, in undertone, *his* Brutus the Liberator, ready to chime with the echo of the Tyrannicide in Clio's next item, 'the noble death of Cato' (vv. 35f.).

Cato's suicide is good to think with (like Hercules' self-immolation): his ancestor's plebeian *nouitas* served Rome in war, in memorializing the history of the *imperium*, in senatorial and censorial severity; Cato's inheritance led him, as it led Brutus, to proud emulation, to end in his case with 'an aristocrat's death', 'a defiant Stoic's self-chosen last blow for freedom' (*nobile letum*). Would his forefather Cato the Censor not have seen himself in his namesake?

Horace finds good cause to think that we can find Rome, find Rome(s) to praise, through exercising our cultural competence in historical legend, in its intrication with the political events that framed his lifetime, just as it frames this poem. But we must continue to allow for the likelihood that echoes, and feed-back noise, can be as important as the names he names.

As we have seen, the run of names through the next two verses reads as a continuation of Clio's dilemma (vv. 37–8). Once we reach the next verb, however, we must convert the list back from *Fabriciumque* (v. 40) through *-que. . . Paulum*, to the *Scauros* and *Regulum* (vv. 38– 7).

It finally becomes clear that *gratus* (thankful) Horace has taken over from Clio (questioned in v. 2; answering in v. 13 and performing at vv. 21, 25, 33f.? Or was it Horace all along?). Horace makes us re-read whatever we made of Regulus and co. (and Romulus and co.?), by making them echo round our heads:

> *quietum* / ~
> *-que magnae* /, vv. 33, 37
> *an Catonis* / ~
> *-am Camena* /, vv. 35, 39.

And a similar effect is achieved by his representing them as positive subjects whose 'recounting' is sure to 'bring pleasure' to him/us, through the ministrations of a Latin 'Muse—with medals' (*re-feram*; *gratus, insigni. . . Camena*, v. 39). This is our modal prompt both to wonder how the candidates for praise we have been considering may best be ranked, and to be assured that the poetry we are helping to reverberate will bestow and merit honour as well as being enjoyed.

Virgil's **Cato** was also pushed forward with strong modality: 'Who could leave you silenced, *magne Cato*?' (v. 841). Anchises set off the interminable debate over Catonian greatness (Which was 'the great Cato'—'Cato the Elder', or was he (merely) 'Great Cato'? Should we reserve *Cato m a i o r* for the 'greater' Cato, the Tyrannicide *Uticensis*?). The maiden-speeches of Cato the tribune-elect of the Catilinarian year were just the start of a meteoric and unprecedented career on his hind legs in the *curia*, and he quickly became the best filibusterer in Roman history since the Censor, who most famously never 'left in silence' the destruction of Carthage. So these orators would stage between them the noisiest ding-dong ever heard by free Rome. No lover of liberty could be cowed from mentioning *them* in praise (or at least *one* of them. . .).

For Horace, though, Cato's last was his proudest moment, monarch of the Self, since until then his arguably (ig)noble sword was turned against the first *Caesar*, and but for his suicide he might have gone the way of Brutus. He would then have blurred his memory from what *he* might consider the end of the Republic, but others preferred to see as the end of the Civil War(s). With Brutus and Tyrannicide, there began the second story of the sequel *Caesar*. Just as 'Tarquin' inaugurated the Republic, so 'Cato' heralded its Augustan 'restitution', in both cases through the intervention of a Brutus. . .

We are now in a position to see that Horace has shown us what is put in play by the difficult project of ordering Roman heroism into a hierarchy. He has put us singer-readers through the process of learning how to love Rome through meditating the historicality of *exempla* in their patterned inter-connections, whether spoken or *sotto uoce*. Now the poet is ready to substitute an echo-stanza which has a rising curve of confidence.

Like Cato, *Regulus* was great in his voluntary death, as great a *regnum* as Numa's, as great as the soul of **Paulus**, and just as great a paradox, too, as a Princeling to go with the diminutive **Cato Minor** and 'Titch' *Paulus* (no match for the 'looming' Hannibal in height, *Paulum* ↔ *superante Poeno*, vv. 35–8). Each threw it all away, in a 'short' moment apiece, in proof of the 'magnanimity' of heroism (in Greek, *megathumia*, 'greatness of soul', ~ the echolalic *animae. . . magnae*, v. 37).

The playful word-name-fame image-factory lists these losers, Regulus and Paulus, both martryred 'when the Carthaginian was the winner'. When their successor arrives next, the Pyrrhic loser-victor / *Fabriciumque*, some ears might hear / *Fabriciumque* (v. 40), since Paulus' moment of self-sacrifice ensured that his disaster at Cannae would blur into another 'ironic' turning-point in history. It brought forth *Fabius*, and his famously attritional negative strategy. Paulus' Cannae, in this sense, eventually turned the tables on Hannibal, with Roman invasion and conquest in Africa, where both Cato and Regulus laid down their lives. Regulus' and Paulus' (very different) tragic sacrifices bound Rome to the death-culture mysticism of never-say-die determination.

Already, Horace's Italian Muse turns to block out a chunk of less kamikaze characters, with frugal **Fabricius** (the conqueror/punch-bag of Pyrrhus, who completed the Roman domination of Italy) another hero who fought off 'alien' invasion of the fatherland, himself invading the stanza's run of devotional 'squanderers' (of self). They already themselves invaded the *last* stanza, as Cato was perched on a throne alongside the kings to contest the truth of 'nobility' (i. e. . . . *regnum? fasces? letum?*).[182]

Now C. **Fabricius** Luscinus, as 'one-eyed' (*luscus*) as that 'Carthaginian' Hannibal, brings his resonant *nomen*, to do more work than form a bulky bridgehead into the next stanza: this *imago* fabricates its welcome joke/encomium by amplifying the word-smith Horace's promise that his pleasurable work of 'representation' is under way (*referam*). The figure of this artisan *Fabricius* fetches with him a statuesque model, who will make his 'well-versed' image stand out 'proud and famous' (*insigni. . . Camena*).

Fabricius is joined by a pair of further antique *imagines*. M'. **Curius** Dentatus was another hero aginst Pyrrhus, but had earlier defeated the Sabines and Samnites. With M. Furius **Camillus** we slip back a further century, to complete the Roman conquest of Veii and so all the Etruscan name; but also to blur into his rescue of Rome from the jaws of Gallic obliteration and his 'second founding' of the city, an Augustus *avant la lettre*.

The Sapphic song/Muse plays chords, still, in our ears:

capillis /,
Camillum / (vv. 41f., cf. *Catonis /*, *Camena /*; / *utilem*).

But it/she works, too, on minds: as we notice that **Curius** is the solitary gentilician *nomen* in the parade, can't we hear the notes that *aren't* played, and supply the 'story' of his *cognomen*?

Curius was personally named *Dentatus* for the 'teeth' he was born with (*dentes*), but, as the epical phrase-epithet draped round him like a Homeric compound adjective intimates, his hair never felt the 'teeth'

110

of a comb because he used his bite in war (*incomptis. . . capillis / utilem bello*; vv. 41f. ; cf. *animae magnae / prodigum* **Paulum**, vv. 37f., for the maxi-honorific 'Homeric' epithet-phrase).

'Sapper' *Fabricius*' pontoons and suchlike of course made *him* useful in war, too: but a *Furius* is obviously best named for battlefield 'Madness' (in Greek, *Mênis*, as in the first word of Homer's *Iliad*). As *Camillus*, however, Furius Camillus' name fits his patriotic military fury as securely as 'his household gods fit his ancestral farm' (vv. 43f.). Hurt by 'savage want', he fought with proportionate savagery (*saeua paupertas*, v. 43); similarly, because he fought for his land, he fought a *holy* fight. *Camillus* condenses all this into the *cognomen*, which names (as we saw) the aristocratic 'boy-ministrant' at priestly sacrifices.[183] 'Aptitude' and 'aptness' are words that regularly occur when fame is awarded or denied (*apto /* and */ cum* join *lare* to *fundus*: so does *auitus*). Here the Roman hymn mellows into the traditional agricultural pieties of the dynastic Roman *domus*.

This train of 'greatness' (*magnae*, v. 37) will shortly settle all these luminaries into the inferior status of humble dependants orbiting around the Julian star (*minores*, v. 48; cf. *inter omnis /↔ inter ignis /*, vv. 46f.). An echo-duo of similes will stealthily/flashily produce a crescendo climax that reaches up to address the Almighty, himself father of our species' *gens* and son of *Saturnus*, spitting image of 'sowing' (*uelut. . . uelut*; *occulto ↔ micat*). For 'a fittingly lowly household *lar* watched over the old farm of the *colonus* Camillus. . . and on it there grew, over the generations, the family-tree of the famous-name **Marcellus**' (vv. 45f.).

This word-image has the 'ring' (*fama*) of a hyper-diminutive (< *Marcus*),[184] but without changing a letter, time has 'grown' acorn into oak (*crescit*, v. 45), and the family fame has extended from (plebeian, *coss.* V) M. Claudius **Marcellus**, whom Virgil's Anchises superadded to *his* parade as 'towering over all the heroes, joint-conqueror (with Fabius and Scipio) of Hannibal,[185] and as punisher of the Gauls, Rome's last winner of the *spolia opima*' (*Aen.* 6. 855–9), on to the proliferation of consular Marcelli of the Late Republic.

Anchises will trail from the generalissimo to his namesake, Augustus' son-in-law **Marcellus**, who would become the tragic first occupant of the mausoleum Augustus had built for himself on the Campus Martius in the same year that Horace's collection of *Odes* was finished. However exactly the times of writing and dying compared, and whatever that thought would make Horace's hymn say, Marcellus the 'son' of Augustus blurs us into the dazzle of the *Iulium sidus*, the star which attests the ascension of *Diuus Iulius*, and so the filial piety of the terrestrial Cosmocrat Augustus (vv. 46f.).

With the Claudii Marcelli, the *Ode*'s list is closed (as is the *Aeneid*'s), and the song, having rattled off its ludic images of a Rome which parades elusive riddles of power (far eclipsed by the effulgence of its triumphant 'Jove'), is ready to subordinate Augustus, finally, to the Master of Olympus, and so to make 'a happy planet'. Even so, the fun whispers, just at the threshold of audibility, that 'this Caesar is a match for his overlord' (*te minor laetum reget aequus orbem*, v. 57).

This, then, is the context within which the (not-so-)generalizing plural *Scauros* means (v. 37).

[i]   In history, between *Regulum* and *animae magnae / prodigum Paulum* came M. *Aemilius* **Scaurus** (*cos.* 115), a century after even Hannibal. *Triumphator* and the last republican *princeps senatus*, Aemilius Scaurus was as famously frugal as Fabricius and Curius; he was as severe as Cato, Regulus, or Paulus, but after the unsparing fashion of the first Brutus, for *he* made one son kill himself for cowardice in action against the Cimbri, the other being a prodigal pleasure-seeker.

[ii] His rival, however, M. *Aurelius* **Scaurus**, was captured by the same Cimbri. His advice for them was not to attack the invincible Romans. For this he was savagely slain.

So, to name *Scauros* on the roll-call of Roman heroism works better if gentilician relatedness is *dis*regarded. Then two contemporaries who fortuitously bore the same nickname fight it out between themselves, or share the honours.

Aurelius's *story* sits well with Regulus; Aemilius is as *Aemilian* as L.

112

Aemilius Paulus: *his* African exploit was to face down and humble Jugurtha as head of the delegation from Rome.[186]

But Horace's Muse is still playing those Italian tricks with word-image-name-fame, even as she inserts (the) *Scauros* between 'Regulus' and 'the soul-greatness of wastrel Paulus', between 'Prince' and 'Shorty' (/ *Regulum et Scauros* rhyming, as we saw, with / *Romulum post hos*, vv. 37, 33). A *Regulus* would lead *Scauros* because *Reguli* are as a rule 'straight as a ruler' (*regula*), which helped to nickname Regulus 'Serranus' for the straightness of his furrows.[187] Whereas *Scauri* have irregular 'swollen ankles' and so totter about precariously on bad legs.[188]

Scauri reverberate in dissonance from *animae magnae* because the nickname, an ill-sorted importation from hippiatrics and the solitary Hellenism in this list, is so evidently an *imago* of the *body*. The name *Scaurus* is a stigmatization, like *Paulus*, which a father must mean his son to rise above in the triumph of his life. These babes were named for foals 'with deviant hooves': they will need big hearts to walk straight and tall.

This summary reading has set out the argument that the subsumption of plurality within a unified collective or regulated system is the very principle of Horace's hymn. Yet this ordering separates into clusters, pairs, doubles. It is tentative and suggestive, blurred and polyrhythmic. It asserts an imagistic parallelism between its dyad of dynamic power-regimes, even while gods blur through heroes into humans, and as the human is subjected to the divine. It blurs the boundaries between these statuses, and confuses the 'original' with its 'copy'.

The poem promises and delivers a lesson in the articulation of praise, both by each choice of name/image/fame, and by the aura and penumbra of evocations and relationships which those choices, and the traces they represent, awaken. The poem itself resounds, as it re-envisions. Its language plays very serious, frivolously irrational and opportunist, ideological mind-games with the reader-singer's cultural competence.

In these games, individuality dances in and out of the grasp of the patriarchally generalizing collective. Where the divine twins, the 'Dioscuri' (*pueros Ledae*), provided a *locus* where the pull of 'oneness' fought to overcome disjunction through the law of paternity, the plural *Scauros* is a very specific place where *gens* may vie, or ally, with *gens*. Or a cultural place where one *gens* may prefer to obliviate its plurality; to 'generalize' from its unique and solitary jewel; and to allow *ciues* to stand side by side for the overriding *gens Romana* (even the *gens humana*).

APPENDIX 2

VIRGIL'S ROLL-CALL OF ROMAN *EXEMPLA*: AENEID 6. 808–86, SYNOPSIS, TEXT AND TRANSLATION

To give an idea of its economy, rhythm and structuring, here is an outline synopsis of the whole 'Roll-call of Heroes' speech of Anchises (Virg. *Aen.* 6. 756–886). The heroes presented by Anchises who are important for Horace, *Odes* 1. 12, and for Juvenal 8, all appear in short stretches within the overall speech. The key passage is vv. 808–86, for which text and translation are given below.

1 SYNOPSIS

[i]   vv. 756–9: Proem. Anchises announces his inspirational programme.

[ii.a] vv. 760–76: Welcome of the Kings of Aeneas' city of Alba Longa: Silvius (vv. 763–6), Procas (v. 767), Capys (v. 768), Numitor (v. 768), Silvius Aeneas (vv. 768–70). The group is enthused over (vv. 772–6).

[ii.b] vv. 777–87: Numitor's grandson is tacked on: Romulus, acclaimed founder and first King of Rome.

[iii.a] vv. 788–90: Parade of the *gens Iulia*: Caesars and all the descent of Iulus (vv. 788–9).

115

[iii.b] vv. 791–807: This introduces Augustus Caesar, annunciated as founder of Golden Ages to come, and as world-conqueror far beyond the range of Hercules (*Alcides*, vv. 801–3) and Bacchus (*Liber*, vv. 804f.).

[iv.a] vv. 808–17: The rest of the Kings of Rome arrive: [Numa] (vv. 808–12), Tullus (vv. 812–5), Ancus (vv. 815f.), the Tarquins (v. 817).

[iv.b] vv. 818–825: This blurs into Heroes of the Republic, from Brutus the founder of the Republic (vv. 817–23), to Decii (v. 824), Drusi (v. 824), Torquatus (vv. 824f.), Camillus (v. 825).

[iv.c] vv. 826–35: [Caesar] and [Pompey] are emotively featured in this list.

[iv.d] vv. 836–46: More Heroes of the Republic march past: [Mummius] (vv. 836f.) and [Aemilius Paullus] (vv. 838–40), Cato (v. 841), Cossus (v. 841), the Gracchi (v. 842), Scipiones (vv. 842f.), Fabricius (vv. 843f.), Regulus Serranus (v. 844). The list culminates in the Fabii and Fabius Maximus Cunctator (vv. 845f.).

[v] vv. 847–53: Impassioned paraenesis to all Romans seems to conclude the speech.

[vi] v. 854: A 'surprise supplement' intervenes:

[vii.a] vv. 855–9: Marcellus.

[vii.b] vv. 860–7: Prodded by Aeneas, Anchises adds a tearful post-script:

[vii.c] vv. 868–86: Marcellus, the adoptive son of Augustus, is hailed and mourned.

2 TEXT

[iv. a] *quis procul ille autem ramis insignis oliuae*   808
sacra ferens? nosco crinis incanaque menta
regis Romani primam qui legibus urbem   810
fundabit, Curibus paruis et paupere terra
missus in imperium magnum. cui deinde subibit

116

otia qui rumpet patriae residesque mouebit
Tullus in arma uiros et iam desueta triumphis
agmina. quem iuxta sequitur iactantior **Ancus**   815
nunc quoque iam nimium gaudens popularibus auris.
uis et **Tarquinios** reges animamque superbam
[iv. b] ultoris **Bruti**, fascisque uidere receptos?
consulis imperium hic primus saeuasque securis
accipiet, natosque pater noua bella mouentis   820
ad poenam pulchra pro libertate uocabit,
infelix, utcumque ferent ea facta minores:
uincet amor patriae laudumque immensa cupido.
quin **Decios Drusosque** procul saeuumque securi
aspice **Torquatum** et referentem signa **Camillum**.   825
[iv. c] illae autem paribus quas fulgere cernis in armis,
concordes animae nunc et dum nocte premuntur,
heu quantum inter se bellum, si lumina uitae
attigerint, quantas acies stragemque ciebunt,
aggeribus socer **Alpinis** atque arce **Monoeci**   830
descendens, gener aduersis instructus **Eois**!
ne, pueri, ne tanta animis adsuescite bella
neu patriae ualidas in uiscera uertite uiris;
tuque prior, tu parce, genus qui ducis **Olympo**,
proice tela manu, sanguis meus!—   835
[iv. d] ille triumphata **Capitolia** ad alta **Corintho**
uictor aget currum caesis insignis **Achiuis**,
eruet ille **Argos Agamemnoniasque Mycenas**
ipsumque **Aeaciden**, genus armipotentis **Achilli**,
ultus auos **Troiae** templa et temerata **Mineruae**.   840
quis te, magne **Cato**, tacitum aut te, **Cosse**, relinquat?
quis **Gracchi** genus aut geminos, duo fulmina belli,
Scipiadas, cladem **Libyae**, paruoque potentem
Fabricium uel te sulco, **Serrane**, serentem?
quo fessum rapitis, **Fabii**? tu **Maximus** ille es,   845
unus qui nobis cunctando restituis rem.

117

[v]   *excudent alii spirantia mollius aera,*
       credo equidem, uiuos ducent de marmore uultus,
       orabunt causas melius, caelique meatus
       describent radio et surgentia sidera dicent: 850
       tu regere imperio, Romane, memento
       (hae tibi erunt artes), pacique imponere morem,
       parcere subiectis et debellare superbos.'
[vi]   *sic pater Anchises atque haec mirantibus addit:*
[vii. a]*aspice, ut insignis spoliis* **Marcellus** *opimis*   855
       ingreditur uictorque uiros supereminet omnis.
       hic rem Romanam magno turbante tumultu
       sistet eques, sternet Poenos Gallumque rebellem,
       tertiaque arma patri suspendet capta Quirino.'
[vii. b]*atque hic Aeneas (una namque ire uidebat*   860
       egregium forma iuuenem et fulgentibus armis,
       sed frons laeta parum et deiecto lumina uultu)
       'quis, pater, ille, uirum qui sic comitatur euntem?
       filius, anne aliquis magna de stirpe nepotum?
       qui strepitus circa comitum! quantum instar in ipso!   865
       sed nox atra caput tristi circumuolat umbra.'
       tum pater Anchises lacrimis ingressus obortis:
[vii. c] *'o nate, ingentem luctum ne quaere tuorum;*
       ostendent terris hunc tantum fata neque ultra
       esse sinent. nimium uobis Romana propago   870
       uisa potens, superi, propria haec si dona fuissent.
       quantos ille uirum magnam Mauortis ad urbem
       campus aget gemitus! uel quae, Tiberine, uidebis
       funera, cum tumulum praeterlabere recentem!
       nec puer Iliaca quisquam de gente Latinos   875
       in tantum spe tollet auos, nec Romula quondam
       ullo se tantum tellus iactabit alumno.
       heu pietas, heu prisca fides inuictaque bello
       dextera! non illi se quisquam impune tulisset
       obuius armato, seu cum pedes iret in hostem   880
       seu spumantis equi foderet calcaribus armos.

118

heu, miserande puer, si qua fata aspera rumpas!
tu Marcellus eris. manibus date lilia plenis,
purpureos spargam flores, animamque nepotis
his saltem accumulem donis, et fungar inani   885
munere.'   886

3 TRANSLATION

[iv. a] 'Who is that, now, in the distance, notable for his olive
    branch,   808
    And the tools for sacrifice? I recognize the hair and
    grizzled chin
    Of the King of Rome who with laws will found   810
    The city, come from tiny Cures, no land of plenty,
    On a mission to command a great empire. Then there will
    succeed him
    The one who will disturb his country's peace and stir
    lounging
    Warriors to arms, and brigades now unaccustomed to
    Triumphs: **Tullus**. Next after him follows **Ancus** the big
    boaster,   815
    Already right now, as well, swooning over the swell of
    popularity.
    Won't you see, too, the **Tarquin** Kings, and the proud soul
[iv. b] of **Brutus** The Avenger, and the vindication of the *fasces*?
    He will be first with the command of the consul and its
    savage axes,
    First to have them authorized, and this father, when his
    sons stir armed revolution,   820
    Will summon them to pay the price, for the beauty of
    freedom,
    Ill-starred—however later generations will regard this deed
    of his:
    There shall prevail love of country, and boundless desire
    for acclamation.

119

But, why!, the **Decii** and **Drusi**, in the distance, and savage
with his axes
See **Torquatus**, and, returning the standards, **Camillus**. 825
[iv. c] Now, those you see gleaming in matching armour,
Spirits in harmony at present, and so long as the dark
holds them down,
Alas, what a great war between them, if once the light of
life
Reaches them, what great battle-lines and carnage they will
herald,
The father-in-law from the rampart Alps, lonely
Monoecus' citadel, 830
Bearing down on the son-in-law drawn up opposite with
the forces of the Dawn!
No! Boys, No! Don't get such great wars used to being in
your hearts,
Don't turn powerful might against your country's womb.
And you first, mercy, you who trace your line from
Olympus,
Throw down the spears from your hand, blood of
mine—! 835
[iv. d] That one, when triumph over Corinth reaches the summit
of Capitol,
Will drive his chariot in victory, special for his slaughter of
Achaean Greeks;
The next will topple Argos and Agamemnon's city of
Mycenae,
And the descendant of Aeacus, no less, off-shoot of
Achilles, lord of combat,
Avenging Troy's grandfathers, and the desecration of
Minerva's precinct. 840
Who could leave you to silence, great **Cato**, and **Cossus**?
Who the **Gracchan** lineage, or the pair, twin bolts of war,
Those **Scipios**, ruination for Libya, and—powerful on the
basis of not much—

Fabricius, or you, **Serranus**, sowing straight down the furrow?
Where are you bundling off this tired one, **Fabii**?—*You* are *the* **Fabius Maximus**, 845
By doing nothing in a hurry, you single-handed restore our state.

[v] Others will hammer out bronze statues that draw breath more delicately,
As I believe, and from the marble beckon living faces expressive as life;
They will plead cases better, and the trajectories across the sky
Will be mapped by their compasses, as they tell the rising of the stars: 850
But do you, man from Rome, remember to govern the nations with your rule,
(These will be your talents) and to imprint the Roman way on peace;
Show mercy once resistance is over; eliminate the entire capability of the uncowed.'

[vi] So father Anchises did speak, and as they marvelled he added:

[vii. a] 'Look: how **Marcellus**, picked out by the *de luxe* spoils he won, 855
Steps out, the conqueror who stands proud of all his heroes.
This man will set the Roman state amid the disturbance of a great panic
To rights, on his mount, then rout Carthage and waste each rebel Gaul,
And hang up the third set ever of captured armour for Father Quirinus.'

[vii. b] And it was at this point Aeneas, because he could see in this company 860
An outstanding, lovely, young man, in dazzling armour,

121

Though his brow was cheerless and his eyes had a
downcast look—
Said, 'Who, father, is this one, who escorts the hero on his
way like this?
His son, or just one of the grandsons from his mighty
stock?
What a rumpus from the mates around him! A great mould
he makes for them all!   865
But black night hovers round his head, in grim shadow.'
Then father Anchises started up, tears welling:
[vii. c] 'O son, don't ask about the vast grief of your family.
Deathstiny will give the earth but a glimpse of him, then
no longer
Permit his existence. The stock of Rome seemed to
you too   870
Powerful, gods of heaven, if this gift had become yours.
Beside the great city of Mars, how much will that plain
Draw groans from heroes! Tiber, you'll see such
A funeral, when you swirl past the fresh pyre!
No boy from the Trojan tribe will ever in Italy   875
Exalt his grandfathers' hopes so high, nor in time to come
will Romulus'
Land pride itself so much on any other nursling.
Alas for his respectfulness! Alas for his old-fashioned
honesty! His invincible
Hand in war! No man would ever have come up to him
Face-to-face for combat, whether he was bound for the foe
on foot,   880
Or was digging spurs into his sweating mount's flanks.
Alas for you, boy—the pity you are due!—if only you
shatter your cruel deathstiny!
You shall be **Marcellus**. Offer lilies, hands full:
I shall scatter purple flowers, and my grandson's spirit
I shall heap with this gifts, at least, to perform the vain 885
Rite.'   886

APPENDIX 3

FABIUS MAXIMUS IN VIRGIL, LIVY, OVID: DISCUSSION (WITH TEXTS AND TRANSLATIONS)

Virgil dramatizes best of all the tug-of-war in being a Fabius. Fabii must try to live up to the contrary injunctions to be dashing for another debonair Cremera, and to dawdle for another Hannibalic deadening delay.

With his Fabius scene, Virgil hurries along to finish off the roll-call text and be done—only for Anchises to carry on delaying *his son*. First with his own paternal precepts to this soon-to-be *Romane* (vv. 847–53). Then with the supplementary arrival of Marcellus, which prompts Aeneas to conspire in the delaying tactics, as well, by questioning him about his look-alike namesake.[189] The book has still some mileage before it is done.

Anchises broke off his roll-call for unnamed apostrophe to Caesar and Pompey. Then he indicated Mummius *Achaicus*[190] and Paullus *Macedonicus*, to be guessed by their *res gestae*. Anchises asks, 'Who could leave you to silence, Cato and Cossus?', but leaves their exploits to silence.[191] Then he leaves out (the word) 'leave', and asks, 'Who [ ] the Gracchan lineage or Scipios, and Fabricius or you Regulus?'. His interrogative form runs on, as he resumes his apostrophe to these

Lethaean characters-to-be in search of an author: *Quo fessum rapitis, Fabii?* The commotion attracts his attention to this 'tired one being bundled off by the Fabii': *tu Maximus ille es, / unus qui nobis cunctando restituis rem* (vv. 826–46, 'You are the famous Fabius Maximus, who single-handed restore our state by doing nothing in a hurry'). These fabled up-and-at-'em Fabii, the 306 of the Roman 'Light Brigade', would whisk *Cunctator* off. . . to die with them by the Cremera; but he is 'tired out' *already*, not yet up to bearing arms in a charge for *uirtus* (like the Greek equivalent, *andreia*, this term emphasizes 'adult manliness', as in the first word of Homer's *Odyssey*).[192] His survival instinct saved Rome—but also saved his clan from its urge for extinction. And not for the last time, as the adoptions of *Aemilianus* and *Seruilianus* later remind us.[193]

Not yet grown, Virgil's Fabius, but 'very big' for his age: Anchises the seer can see the future Greatestness of 'Maximus'. How tragically inside-out the troop of Marcelli by contrast: there the Punic War hero **Marcellus** will march up 'taller by far than all the rest, loaded in victory with his *spolia opima*'. And, Anchises sees, *hic rem Romanam. . . sistet* ('this man will set to rights the Roman state'). But the Marcellan crowd also masses round a single unique adolescent descendant.

Fabius will spell 'exhaustion' for the meaning of his life, but Princel-ing **Marcellus** brings 'downcast sadness'. Fabius was warty, Marcellus a lovely young man. Fabius couldn't go fight Veii, Marcellus' arms boast parade-ground polish. Fabius learns to resist and tame adrenalin, even as his companions tug at him; Marcellus and company are at one in comradely harmony. Fabius *looks* as though he must be a grave disappointment to his parents;[194] some father has trained Marcellus perfectly. Yet all the Fabii die, so that Maximus can cunctate, whereas all the Marcelli triumph down the years, so that they can escort Marcellus straight to an early death without glory, far from the front. And this 'sole and unique' chip off the old Marcellan block would have inherited all the clan's estate, in fact, the whole World State, if only he had lived.

What Virgil does by writing Fabius into his catalogue is make him a 'false' *Abbruchsformel* (rhetorical formula for breaking off a theme, ready to launch into a new direction). Fabius is, in fact, a purpose-made traditional figure for a climax. He was used in Ennius' *Annales* 12 to look back on an age of heroes,[195] just as Juvenal uses his *Fabius* to climax his series of harangues, before he debouches into that all-embracing 'answer' of his (*Sat.* 8. 13–8 ↔ 19f.).

Ovid's version of the saga of the Fabian clan's suicidal patriotism at the Cremera also ends with the boy *meant* to survive:

> *scilicet ut posses olim* **tu, Maxime,** *nasci,*
> *cui res cunctando restituenda foret.* // (Ov. *Fast.* 2. 241–2).

> So that, no doubt, you, Maximus, might one day be born,
> Who would have to restore the state by delaying.[196]

But Ovid's story continues, to the next day on the calendar, delayed by a story of delay, until the drawn-out Luperci story reveals (in a flash) its strategic role as another way of boxing clever for Fabian fame.[197]

And (we just saw) Virgil's story continues, too, past Anchises' strongly closural *mandata*, straight into the Marcelli 'sequel', and, at the grandest level of all, in the entire narrration of the *Aeneid*. For Virgil's text 'roll-calls' Roman heroes, before Aeneas and before its readers, in a *longo ordine* which is organized under the figure *longo sanguine* ('long row ~ long blood<line>'). Epic hands us what matters, namely Rome, by dwelling on its theme, covering the paper, holding out for more of the reader's time, tiring out any audience, too short of wind to keep the pace up with Aeneas and the Muse, unready for devotional survival through reading. The epic Fabius stares down (at) the next weedy contender, figured by Anchises as 'the one', the one who can best 'stand' for Rome, for Virgil's Rome.

For Livy, too, *Cunctator* was the rare son who in surpassing *his* father(s), showed how special the pleading must be, before *le nom du pére*, how little chance sons *of a father such as himself* must stand of achieving this. His acute *elogium* runs:

> *superauit paternos honores, auitos aequauit. pluribus uictoriis et maioribus proeliis auus insignis Rull<ian>us; sed omnia aequare unus hostis Hannibal potest* (Liv. A.U.C. 30. 26. 8).

125

He outdid his father's *c.v.*, and matched granddad's. Grandfather Rullianus was famous for more victories and greater battles; but just the one foe Hannibal can square up the whole score.

This is what Juvenal uses his Fabii to bring out, for all us imaginary *Pontici*. Fabius Maximus and the Fabii are supposed to be a hard act to follow, none harder.

Thus when Ovid's *auxesis* (rhetorical amplification) means to extol the greatness of (the name) *Augustus*, he builds his rhetoric around outdoing the apparently ultimate superlative title of the Fabii Maximi:

Idibus in magni castus Iouis aede sacerdos	587
semimaris flammis uiscera libat ouis;	
redditaque est omnis populo prouincia nostro	
*et tuus **Augusto** nomine dictus auus.*	590
perlege dispositas generosa per atria ceras:	
contigerunt nulli nomina tanta uiro.	
Africa** uictorem de se uocat, alter **Isauras	
*aut **Cretum** domitas testificatur opes;*	
*hunc **Numidae** faciunt, illum **Messana** superbum,*	595
*ille **Numantina** traxit ab urbe notam:*	
*et mortem et nomen Druso **Germania** fecit;*	
me miserum, uirtus qua breuis illa fuit!	
*si petat a uictis, tot sumat nomina **Caesar***	
quot numero gentes maximus orbis habet.	600
*ex uno quidam celebres aut **torquis** adempti*	
*aut **corui** titulos auxiliaris habent.*	
***Magne**, tuum nomen rerum est mensura tuarum:*	
sed qui te uicit nomine maior erat.	
*nec gradus est supra **Fabios** cognominis ullus:*	605
*illa domus meritis **Maxima** dicta suis.*	
sed tamen humanis celebrantur honoribus omnes,	
hic socium summo cum Ioue habet.	
*sancta uocant **augusta** patres, **augusta** uocantur*	
templa sacerdotum rite dicata manu:	610

huius et augurium dependet origine uerbi
et quodcumque sua Iuppiter auget ope.
augeat imperium nostri ducis, augeat annos,
protegat et uestras querna corona fores:
auspicibusque deis tanti cognominis heres   615
omine suscipiat, quo pater, orbis onus! (Fast. 1. 587–616).[198]

On the Ides the celibate priest in the shrine of great Jove   587
  Offers the flames the guts of a castrated ram;
And every province was restored to our people,
  Your grandfather was acclaimed with his **Augus**tan name.   590
Read through the wax (images) arranged through the *atria* of the
  nobility:
No names of comparable magnitude have befallen any of the
  heroes.
Africa calls her conqueror after herself; someone else gives
  Isaurian,
Or **Cretans'** power his attestation, now he has broken them;
One the **Numidians,** another **Messana** makes proud,   595
And this one drew his label from the city of **Numantia,**
While **Germany** brought Drusus both death and famous name;
  How sad that his courage was so brief!
If **Caesar** went for titles from defeated peoples, he would take as
  many
  In number as the greatest extent of the world contains.   600
From just one foe some became famous, either for the **collar** one
  took,
  Or for the **raven** that came to aid another, whence their
  christening.
You, 'The Great', your name is the measure of your achievements:
  But the one who defeated you was greater still in name.
Likewise, there is no further degree of epithet beyond the
  superlative of the **Fabii;**   605
  Thanks to their efforts that household has been dubbed 'The
  Greatest'.

127

But for all that all these are fêted with human honours:
The one we mean has a name that allies him with highest Jove.
Our fathers call what is holy 'august', 'august' is what temples
 Are called, when properly dedicated by a priest's hand: 610
'Augury' stems from the base of the same word,
 Plus whatever Jove **augments** with his power.
May he **augment** the empire of our leader, and **augment** his span,
 And may the crown of oak-leaves defend your door:
Auspiciously backed by the gods, may the heir to so great a
 title   615
Take up the burden of the globe, with the same omens as did
 his father!   616

Ovid here collects all the examples he can to focus on the challenge/threat to Roman political discourse of accommodating the requisite supervenience of the new Emperor figure within the traditions of Republican honorific titulature. He fits in all the examples, and avers that Caesar could assume all the triumphal *agnomina* in the *maximus orbis*. *Magnus* was only 'great', his conqueror was *maior* (greater). So we might suppose that there can be no degree of *cognomen* beyond the Fabii, and their *domus* called *maxima* (the greatest). And we would be right, too. Except, that is, for the super-human *summus* Jove, who shares his ally's name *Augustus*. This is the same mytho-logic that structures Horace's *Ode* 1. 12, a classic Augustan paradigm for extension of praise to the modest exorbitance of the self-styled paternal *Princeps*. Rome needed to construct a place for Augustus in Latin.

More generally, too, the role in the rhetoric of praise which positions Fabii Maximi as ultimate *non pareils*, before hitting on a path toward transcending them, is precisely how both poetry and history honoured them. For if Fabius was the saviour, Scipio won the war; *Maximus* at least lived up to his superlative (ancestors') name-fame-story—but a new *style* of title was found for *Africanus*. Thus Livy's Third Decade does lift itself to epic sublimity to commemorate Fabius:

*nihil certius est quam 'unum hominem nobis cunctando rem resti-
tuisse', sicut Ennius ait* (Liv. *A. U. C.* 30. 26. 9).

Nothing's more certain than that 'the man single-handed restored our
state by doing nothing in a hurry', as Ennius has it.[199]

But the narrative of course continues, *without* delay, to Scipio's battle
of Zama, and on into the future.

As we have seen, both Virgil's Anchises and Ovid's calendar use this
same 'last word' on Fabius *Cunctator* from Ennius' retrospect to sign
off *their* scenes—and provide the motif for continuing their narration.
In all these cases, and a long line of others besides, the writers make a
strong decision not to spin out, but to cut short, the Ennian *elogium*.
From Cicero, we know that the finality of that final, vindicated
monosyllable *rem.* / was *not* the end of Fabius. For the quotation
continues, with:

ʔnon enimʔ[200] *rumores ponebat ante salutem;*
ergo postque magisque uiri nunc gloria claret (*De Off.* 1. 84, *De Sen.*
10; Enn. *Ann.* 363 Skutsch).

He didn't, ʔyou seeʔ put gossip above survival.
That is why now, ever more the more time goes on, his glory shines
bright.

Did Virgil 'hesitate' to 'whirl on', straight into the teeth of a textual
crux, in the very next word of the citation? Did this next line seem 'too
defensive' for *Cunctator*? Do patriotic narrators such as Anchises
suppress what tells against Fabius, but by their very narration *enact*
what the cut verses asserted—and no need to *say* it? When we read on,
do these excisions shadow the anti-boast, and the precepts, which
displace the lines, and contribute silently toward their reception? And
is this, indeed, the final reflection this book has to offer, in response to
Juvenal's stirring

• *Stemmata quid faciunt?*

- Are even the greatest of past heroes only ever that if their record is doctored, if we can forget their down-side, if we play blind to the manipulation of their legends by people bent on domineering over the present?'

Roll the story on, and you'll find a father's glory is a son bullied. That's the 'truth' of patriarchy. You see, Juvenal *does* have social programming *all* figured out.

APPENDIX 4

GLOSSARY OF ROMAN COGNOMINA: WHY IS A ROMAN EMPEROR LIKE P?[201]

Nb. In this section, as throughout, '<' means 'derived from'.

Augustus: Holy, Well-omened (< *augur*); Augmented (< *augeo*)
Blandus: Sweet-Talker
Brutus: Dumbo, Brute
Buteo: Hawk
Camillus: Altar-Boy
Cicero: Chick-Pea
Coruus/Coruinus: Raven
Crus: Lower Leg
Cunctator: Delayer
Curius: The Senator (<*curia*)
Dentatus: Toothy, Born with Teeth
Dossuo: Hunchback
Drusus: Conqueror of Drausus
Eburnus: Ivory-White
Fabius: Mr Bean (< *faba*); Digger (<*fodio*); The Pits (<*fouea*)
Fabricius: Handyman, Engineer (<*faber*)
Felix: Lucky

Flaminius Priestley
Furius: Maniac
Galba: Grub, i.e. Thin; Fatso (in Gallic?)
Gurges: Abyss, Glutton
Labeo: Rubber-Lips
Lateranus: Bricky (<*later*); Loins (<*latus*)
Lentulus: Slowcoach (<*lentus*); Lentil (< *lens*)
Lepidus: Charmer
Luscinus: One-Eye
Magnus: (The) Great, Mr Big
Maior: Greater, Bigger, Taller, Elder
Marcellus: Little *Marcus*; Martial (<*Mars*)
Maximus: (The) Greatest
Messalla: Conqueror of Messana
Minor: Lesser, Smaller, Younger
Numa: Law (<Greek *nomos*), Holy (<*numen*)
Ouicula: Lambkin
Paul(l)us: Titch
Pictor: Painter
Piso: Pounder (of meal <*pinso*)
Pius: Respectful
Pompilius: Escort (<Greek *pompê*)
Ponticus: Oceanic, Man from Pontus
Priscus: Previous
Regulus: Prince (<*rex*), Ruler (<*regula*)
Rubellius: Blushkin (<*ruber*)
Scaurus: Swollen Ankles (< Greek *skauros*)
Scipio: Stick, Sceptre
Serranus: Straight-Sower (<*sero*)
Sulla: Thin-legged (<*surula*); Sibyl (<*Sibylla*)
Superbus: Proud
Torquatus: Man with the Collar
Verrucosus: Warty
Vindex: The Avenger

NOTES

1 I must thank the general editor of *Exeter Studies in History*, Professor T. P. Wiseman, for his legendary professionalism; and, especially, the anonymous reader who painstakingly saved me from gaffes and lapses to left and to right. The atrocities that are left are all mine.

2 Your a*nts, *ncles and co*sins need 'u' to exist. Dedication: this book is, irreparably, *in mem*. J. S. W. Henderson (1919–95).

3 Braund (1988) 69–129, 'Satire 8: Moralist or Nihilist?' deals authoritatively with the poem's narrator and structure, and its thematic and formal antecedents. Fredericks (1971) vindicates Juvenal's 'poetic skill' with an appreciative reading. Syme (1986) is the key work of reference for any such study as this.

4 And, och aye, one more fall of hame.

5 Most MSS repeat / *Coruinum* from v. 5; / *Fabricium* is an emendation from Renaissance Italy, preferred to modern rivals by the old Oxford Classical text of S. G. Owen.

6 1. 170f., *illos / quorum Flaminia tegitur cinis atque Latina.* Even (especially) road-names were, and are, deposits of gentilician fame (here the *gens Flaminia* < *flamen*, 'priest', aptly covers ritually cremated ashes). Romans knew perfectly well that the traditionalist slant to their cultural ideology meant that the dead were good—indispensable—to

133

think with: Roman epic, history, satire, and art made nearly as much mileage from the play within the indirect implicature of present within representation of the past as any modern nation. Think of Silius Italicus, author of a gargantuan version of the Roman defeat of Hannibal, daring to write Roman Epic at the end of the first century CE, with a cast-iron alibi for blanking from the scene of his text three whole centuries, including his own, the Emperors' era; ask, why *is* pageantry set several centuries in the past so uncomplicatedly attractive? Silius, virtually unread today, will be an important point of reference in this study: Juvenal's 'straight man', or stooge.

7 For the Augustans M. Furius Camillus, *cos.* 8CE, and Q. Sulpicius Camerinus, *cos.* 9CE, cf. Syme (1986) 97f. ; on Q, Sulpicius Quirinius, *cos.* 12CE, cf. Tac. *Ann.* 3. 48. 1, *nihil ad ueterem et patriciam Sulpiciorum familiam Quirinius pertinuit, ortus apud municipium Lanuuium* ('Q. had no bearing on the antique patrician family of Sulpicii: his origin was the township of Lanuvium'), Wiseman (1971) 263 no. 416. To prove the rule, Augustus' right-hand man *Agrippa* dropped his *Vipsanius* gentilician name, a monicker which made him just one from a line of nobodies: he thereby gave himself a 'monarchic' designer profile fit for an imperial deuteragonist (second-in-command); Agrippa would, naturally, have faced incorporation into the *Iulii Caesares* through adoption, had he lived to inherit the Empire.

8 Cf. Mayer (1991), Bloomer (1992) (who somehow steers clear of Juvenal), and refs. in Nisbet and Hubbard on Hor. *Carm.* 1. 12. 37.

9 Stob. *Flor.* 86. 17; cf. Mayor on Juv. 8. 20. It should be obvious that terms such as *nobilitas* and *uirtus* could never settle to the work of mere *calques* (translationese glosses) on approximate equivalents in Greek; they were too embedded and enmeshed in Roman codes for *that*. This essay means to put this beyond a venture.

10 Plin. *Nat. Hist.* 35. 6, in his critical report of the ancestral *imagines* in old Roman *atria*. (See Mayor on 8. 1.)

11 1. 63f, *libet medio ceras implere capaces / quadriuio...*

12 On 1. 1–21, see Henderson (1995).

13 'Another familiar Callimachean opposition is between untrodden paths (untapped subject-matter) and the well-worn highway. Juvenal again

defeats our expectations by choosing the busy highway—to be precise, a crossroads in the heart of Rome (*medio. . . quadriuio*, 63–4)' (Gowers [1993A] 193).

14 Cf. Zanker (1988), esp. 210–3. The seven hundred portraits with couplet-captions in the fifteen books of Varro's *Imagines* mixed the media on paper (Rawson [1985] 198f.: believe it—or not, cf. Skydsgaard [1992]). Sculptural programmes and their descriptions/exegeses contest together in a cultural textuality of norms, ideals, morals—and of their carnivalization; cf. Elsner (1993).

15 On the passage, see Hine (1987), esp. 177f. Others will believe more easily that Virgil means just what he has Anchises say and will draw a dead expression of *recusatio* (gesture of refusal) from this priamel. For my part, I credit the poet with using the material of his rhetorical foil (the preliminary material set aside), which summarizes what Virgil has just *performed* in the shape of Anchises' enlivened march-past of animated statues, to set the topics in which the cap (the point Virgil wants to get across) will bless the Romans with hyper-excellence: to spell this out in brisk paraphrase, Virgil's parade has, precisely, 'remembered the supremacist imperial destiny, with its blend of strategic shifts between imposing the Roman way on those who renounce war, showing mercy once resistance has collapsed, and holding out for unconditional surrender from those unreconciled to subject status. Virgil's skill has just introduced us to these Roman skills, putting the case optimally, mapping out the ascendant stars rising above the rest of the traffic to become the permanent fixtures of eternal Rome. For those heroes implemented the grand strategy, inspired Virgil to memorialize them, and through them, to memorialize it' (vv. 849–53). Don't speak of irony from Anchises *or* Virgil here, but see, instead, how they are presenting to us pupils a model of how to teach by teaching about teaching. We shall consider the false ending to the catalogue of heroes at v. 846 later; for now, notice how utterly critics always manage to forget at this point in their exegesis how they themselves introduced the 'roll-call' by recalling the perambulation of Rome's funereal *imagines*—then pinch yourself.

16 Already from the Augustan aristocracy, 'Some were gone for good.

Nothing could be done for the. . .' (Syme [1986] 77, cf. Tac. *Ann.* 3. 55. 1).

17 For *imagines* in the *atrium*, cf. *RE.* 9. 1097, *Suppl.* 13. 1363. Waxen death masks interacted with painted portraits, sculptured busts, etc. (cf. Sherwin-White on Plin. *Epp*.1. 17. 3). For a review of their art history, cf. Jackson (1987); for their interaction with the theatrical spectacularity of the Roman cultural *ensemble*, see Gregory (1994), esp. 91 on 'the stimulus to action' of Roman ancestral portraits.

18 See the breakthrough study of Salway (1994).

19 Macrob. *Sat.* 1. 77 wants *Sulla* one syllable short < *Sibylla*; Quintil. *Inst. Orat.* 1. 4. 25 hints at < *Surula* = Thin-leggies (*sura*).

20 M. Valerius Maximus *Messalla* < Messana, *cos.* 263, claimed to be the first of these. The *locus classicus* for the triumphal *cognomen* is Ov. *Fast.* 1. 587–616. A text and translation is provided for this in Appendix 3 (pp. 126–8).

21 The protestation goes on, o'ermuch: e. g. Syme (1986) 19, 'Sons of the blood enjoyed no kind of organic or mystical preference. Even malice or folly would not induce an enemy to declare that Aemilianus fell short of an authentic Scipio.' Why, you might find yourself wondering, bother having families at all?

22 Syme (1986) 39, ''Imperator Caesar Divi f. Augustus', anomalous and exorbitant in each member. It was a travesty of any licences of nomenclature practised by the high aristocracy.' (Cf. Syme [1958].)

23 Syme (1960) 12–20.

24 Cf. Salomies (1992).

25 *Tria nomina* ('three names') were rattled out only in some formal contexts. The combination of *praenomen* and *cognomen* carried a marked value of noble status. Grammarians and other commentators who dissect the name-system *promote* the *tria nomina* pattern, which however in no era monopolized or even characterized Roman onomastics (cf. Gallivan [1992]).

26 To give an idea of how dense this kind of name-play can become, let's take a dash through the three etymological plays which come together at Lucan, *Bell. Ciu.* 5. 16, where the consul *Lentulus Crus*, 'enthroned on high' (*e celsa sublimis sede*, 16: [i] *crus* means 'leg below the knee')

'speaks s-l-o-w-l-y' (*profatur*: [ii] *lentus* means 'slow'), cf. Juv. 8. 187, *uelox. . . Lentulus* ['speedy L.'], with Sil. *Pun.* 1. 676–9, *Lentulus. . . celeri. . . bello. / at Fabius, cauta speculator mente futuri* ['L. in swift war, contrast Fabius, cautiously scouting the prospects'], 5. 231–4, *Lentulus. . . nisu se concitat acri* ['L. launched himself with instant energy'], 10. 260ff. and 279–91, *uiolatus harundine plantam / Lentulus... ; consul 'macte o uirtute paterna. . . calcaribus aufer. . . equum atque hinc ocius. . . sed uano quid enim te demoror. . . eripe quadrupedem propere', tum Lentulus...,* ['L., damaged by an arrow in the sole. . . ; the consul said, "Bless you for your ancestral courage,. . . spur your horse away, whip your mount away from here with all speed. . .. But why am I slowing you down with empty. . .'. Then L. . . .']). Lucan's Lentulus Crus speaks for, not just the shins, but the whole body of the senatorial '*part*-y' (*partes*, 14). [iii] The name Lentulus also makes him the (Mendelian) 'Mr Bean' aptly allotted to speak for all the Roman aristocratic prairie-gardeners in the senatorial order (Plin. *Nat. Hist.* 18. 20, *cognomina. . . Pisonis a pinsendo, iam Fabiorum, Lentulorum Ciceronum, ut quisque aliquod optime genus sereret*: 'the *cognomen* Piso is from 'pounding'; the names of the Fabii ['beans'], Lentuli ['beans'], and Cicerones ['chick-peas'], tell how each was best at sowing each species of produce'; cf. Cicero's jibe, *Ad Att.* 1. 19. 2, *to epi tês phakês muron Lentulus* ['L.—the seasoning on the beanstew']. Thus Lucan's Lentulus intones: 'Don't look at the *land* we are driven to, decide we are the senate, if there beat in us hearts of *oak* worthy of Latin *nurture*, of our blood-line'; 'history shows that, wherever transplanted, Roman order survives any change of *soil*. . .' (17–30, cf. the farmer's gear in *plaustrum, axis*, 23f. [waggon, axle]).

27 Syme (1978) 80. See esp. Ov. *Ex Pont.* 3. 6 for a (Brutti/edius) *Brutus* as another dissembling 'dummy' (*brutus*), in the tradition of Iunius Brutus the *Liberator*.

28 Tac. *Ann.* 3. 48: 'born near the town of Lanuvium', this *nouus* rose to *consul* in 12. His *cognomen* made him a comically déclassé replica of Romulus-risen-and-re-christened in heaven as *Quirinus*, particularly in the genitive case: *Quirini*, as in both Tacitus' references to his burial (*ut mors Sulpici Quirini publicis exsequiis frequentaretur. . ., haud laeta*

memoria Quirini ['so the death of Sulpicius Quirinius might be cele-
brated with a state funeral. . . the far from blessed memory of
Quirinius']). Silius dreams up a *Quirinius* for his battle at the River
Ticinus, thereby saluting, by speaking this name-and-fame, the Roman
fatherland's archetypal deified hero in opposition to his Gaul decapita-
tor, who boasts his helmet-full and 'roars salutation to his ancestral gods'
(*patrio diuos clamore salutat, Pun.* 4. 192–215).

29   Tac. *Ann.* 12. 53–4.

30   *Ib.* 12. 1–2, *stirpem nobilem et familiae Iuliae Claudiaeque posteros coniungeret.*

31   At *Bell. Ciu.* 2. 234, *Bruti,* cf. 3. 514, *Bruti.* Brutus the future tyrannicide
preferred to jettison his uncle's adoptive name of Q. Seruilius Caepio
('Some were gone for good. Nothing could be done for the Servilii
Caepiones', Syme [1986] 77f.). Indifference to *Bruti* communicates the
breakdown of order that Lucan's *Bella. . . plusquam ciuilia* ('Civil
War—and worse', 1.1) records and protests.

32   Propertius chose **Ponticus**, composer of a *Thebaid,* as the stooge for his
vindication of love and elegy (1. 7, 9), for much the same web of reasons:
in Greek, *Pontikos sounds* like an aptly 'oceanic' name for the poet of
a vast Homeric epic. There *were Pontici* from various *gentes* in history,
e. g. Tac. *Ann.* 14. 41, *Valerius P.* For further thoughts, see Braund
(1988) 226f. n. 59.

33   E. g. Cornelia in Prop. 4. 11. 11f., **quid mihi coniugium Paulli, quid
currus auorum | profuit. . .?** ('What have my marriage to Paullus and
the triumphal chariot of my grandfathers profited me?').

34   Cf. Suet. *Galb.* 3. 1, *imagines et elogia uniuersi generis exsequi longum
est...* ('It's a long job to go through the *imagines* and honorary plaques
of the whole clan'). *Satire* 8 is longest in *Book* 3, nearly twice the length
of 9, though only a 'page' longer than 7. Not *that* long, however, for
Juvenal (*Satires* 3, 6, 10, 14 are longer).

35   Cf. Sen. *De Ben.* 3. 28. 2, *qui imagines in atrio exponunt et nomina
familiae suae longo ordine ac multis stemmatum illigata flexuris in
prima parte aedium collocant, non noti magis quam nobiles sunt?*
('People who display *imagines* in their hall and set up in the first section
of their home you come to the names of their relatives in a long row,

tied in with many a swerve of the *stemmata*—aren't they well-known rather than noble?'). It is not long before Juvenal puns again: *gaudia longa* (v. 47, 'long joys').

36   1. 162f.

37   Anchises models both Virgil's Augustan evasion of direct explication of his present, and the advantages of an indirect negotiation of that explication, set in the mists of time. The crisis of Silius' Flavian '*Aeneid*' is when *his* Venus-Jupiter primal scene arrives, not after Virgil's two hundred-odd lines, but to round off *Punica* 3, with Hannibal about to cross his Rubicon: Venus' folk will rule for long aeons, but then heavenly *uirtus* will raise itself to the stars from Sabine Cures when a warlike *gens* will augment the *nomen* of the sacred *Iulii*. . . The voice of destiny must skip in a flash from defeat of Hannibal (by v. 592) through the eternity of the Iulii Caesares' line (v. 593), to the advent of the Flavians (from v. 594, / *Exin*. . ., ['at once']), and on to panegyric of Domitian (to v. 629), to supplement Virgil's glimpse of the future: if we thought Anchises' unnamed king to follow Romulus, the Iulii and Augustus Caesar, was *Numa* from *Curibus paruis* (*Aen.* 6. 811), we were wrong, for Virgil never nods; his poem even told the Flavians how to see themselves as always already foretold. The *Punica* keeps buckling under the strain of blanking out all history from Zama to the Domitianic present, to give reader and writer alike the delicious pleasure of consorting with Rome before the fall of the Republic; or (to decode that) the poet will not hide the implications of fleeing with his audience, away to a world of Roman greatness they *can* gladly celebrate: namely that it has obliquely accented implications for the present; for, just as in the *Aeneid*, everything in Silius is, as it were, in italics (cf. Wilson [1993] 234).

38   The poem's weave between description-depiction and discussion-diegesis is loaded toward the latter, but visuality stays strong in the presentation of the whole poem. (Cf. Fowler [1991], on figurality in both modes.)

39   Milton, *Paradise Regained* 2. 445f., quoted by Nisbet and Hubbard on Hor. *Carm.* 1. 12. 40. *Quintius?* This is Cincinnatus.

40   Nisbet and Hubbard on Hor. *Carm.* 1. 12. 37: between them, they

don't, be it said, care for this particular poem—and it shows. My analysis playfully shadows their analysis of 'the generalizing plural' and supports their deconstruction of such analysis. (For further material on the 'generalizing plural', cf. Courtney on Juv. *Sat.* 2. 3.)

41 West (1993) 290 decides: 'Now, every family has skeletons in its cupboards, but there is no call to open all the doors. In interpreting these *exempla*, what is required is not prosopographical research, but simply attention to the whole tone of the context and the whole thrust of the argument.' This weighty pronouncement deserves careful attention. A brief note must suffice. Now, what could persuade anyone at this late epoch to suppose that any 'simpl[e]' form of 'attention' could be adequate to Virgil's visionary text? And, surely, neither a 'context' nor an 'argument' need (ever) have any such characteristic as a 'whole tone' or a 'whole thrust'. Rather, these modal marks from West signal holistic protreptic from another instructor-figure, working to elide from his exegesis the complexity, refraction and contention in the textuality of his exegetical text. Only a devout immanentist could conceivably propound the following political glissando, worthy of Anchises: 'statues. . . erected *by Augustus himself, and therefore not at all subversive*' (*ib.*). West has just rightly imagined Virgil's 'host of Roman families escorting presumably one of their members towards birth and the upper world—a multiple funeral in reverse' (289). These 'families' are the ghosts coming out of the woodwork into the forum at every gentilician funeral; what Romans required to imagine the scene was not prosopographical research, but complex attention to the whole range of tones of the context and the whole thrust toward contestation of the argument. Appeal to 'context' in Virgil or Juvenal provides a frame for reviewing gentilician schemata, but this does not exclude examination of its holistic dynamics: Romans, we know, both could confine *imagines* to 'cupboards' (Tac. *Ann.* 2. 32. 1), and (precisely) knew, without anyone to tell them, that fellow-Romans at least could, on occasion, know how to spot even the 'skeletons' left behind—from their glaring *absence*: 'The *imagines* of twenty families were carried in the van, Manlii, Quinctii, and others of the same nobility. But ahead of them shone out Cassius and Brutus, for the very reason that their likenesses were not to

be seen' (*ib.* 3. 76. 4f., *uiginti clarissimarum familiarum imagines antelatae sunt, Manlii, Quinctii aliaque eiusdem nobilitatis. sed praefulgebant Cassius atque Brutus eo ipso, quod effigies eorum non uisebantur*). As *Aeneid* 6 shows, too, Roman readers knew how to over-read a diminuendo to end a book as a rhetorically amplified blast of litosis (understatement). As Anchises finds, it's not so simple a task to tell even one son what to think, especially about filiation and affiliation.

42 See Goldhill (1994).

43 Because it was his name.

44 *Aemiliani* are found in a large number of *gentes*, but we presume they borrow some fame from Scipio's name, adoptively, maternally, or suppositiously. There were even *Aemilii Aemiliani*.

45 Cf. Polyb. *Hist.* 6. 53f.

46 For the three *gentes'* intertwined stemma, cf. Wiseman (1993) 192; Wiseman (1985) is the classic discussion of élite competition and cooperation at Rome.

47 See Henderson (1988), esp. 199–202.

48 Silius' epic makes the same point by presenting unspecified Scipio after unspecified Scipio—father-and-son (*Pun.* 4. 51, 230; 117), two brothers (7. 106f. ; in the katabasis met by Scipio *filius*, 13. 383f.), or the cousins Nasica and Africanus (17. 10; 48). Manilius inserts determinist theory into his conceit: *Scipiadas. . . duces, fatum Carthaginis unum* (*Astron.* 1. 792, 'the Scipionic leaders, the single deathstiny of Carthage'). Virgil's double twin apposition *geminos, duo fulmina belli, / Scipiadas, cladem Libyae* (*Aen.* 6. 842f., 'twins, two bolts of war, the Scipionics, doom of Libya'), includes (at least) both the Spanish Scipionic casualties and both the Africani, since *cladem Libyae* can metonymically cover Carthaginians in Spain, or indeed anywhere else, and the genitive need not be objective: as Feeney (1986) 14 notes, the demise of Q. Caecilius Metellus Pius Scipio to end (one) Civil War at Thapsus in 46 counts, alongside Africanus' victory over Hannibal's Carthage at Zama, as Lucan's Elysium insists: *deplorat Libycis perituram Scipio terris / infaustam subolem* (*Bell. Ciu.* 6. 788, 'Scipio weeps', not over the ashes of his sacked Carthage, but 'at the funeral of Rome

on Libyan soil which the story of his tears anticipated'). *Pius* Scipio (son of Scipio Nasica, adopted by Metellus Pius, Syme [1986] Tables I, XIX) had worn his *stemmata* far from lightly, for instance erecting what he believed was a statue of his great-grandfather Scipio Nasica Serapio on the Capitol (Cic. *Ad Att.* 6. 1). For 'The Last Scipiones' see Syme (1986) 244–54, Table XIX.

49 **Scipio** as *scipio* = *skêptron* sticks a story in a name: it attests the filial piety of a Cornelius who became his blind father's 'cane' (Maltby [1991] 551, *s.v*). Thus the Scipiadae were born *rulers*, even *before* Ennius (say) sublimated the *skêptron* which put fire in Rome's belly as the Jovian thunder-bolt, *fulmen* ('bolt', < *fulge-men*), bolstered by *fulmen* ('something to lean on', < *fulci-men*, as *skêptron* < *skêptô*; cf. Cic. *Pro Balb.* 34, Sil. *Pun.* 7. 106f., Skutsch [1968] 145–50. Since *Barca* also meant 'lightning', Sil. 15. 664, Hannibal Barca and Scipio fought fire with fire in onomastic *Blitzkrieg*).

50 Silius underlines the *sense* of Virgil's *referentem signa* **Camillum** / (*Aen.* 6. 825: paired with Torquatus and so 'bringing back' the bacon, *not* of the bloody necklace of a Gallic Goliath who lost his head, but of the sacred legionary eagles and the gold captured by the Gauls—and of his own army: *signa*): **Camillus** names a 'diminutive' aristocratic boy-ministrant to the *superi* ('gods above'; cf. Ogilvie on Liv. *A.U.C.* 5. 1. 2. Lucan 6. 786 substitutes Virgil's *referentem s. C.* / with his own *flentem Camillum* /, 'grieving' civil war's *scelus*, 'wickedness'). Lucan's phrase for Curius *non umquam* ('not ever') parades his fidelity to the exemplary tradition, tests his readers' competence to re-wind back to the dawn of Latin time/text with *pater Ennius' Annales*. On *Georg.* 2. 169–72, Thomas too quickly writes off *magnosque Camillos* / ('great Camilli') as a 'poeticism': *Italia* grows this laudable *genus acre uirum* ('fierce breed of men'), planted in a row of producers and weeds between *Decios Marios* and / *Scipiadas. . . et te, maxime Caesar* because *the* Camillus *did* sire a consular son (builder of Iuno Moneta's Mint) who sired a consular son (honoured by the state with a Forum-statue). The stock, as well as the speaking name-and-fame, earned Augustan revival, M. Furius Camillus, *cos.* 8 CE, who then paid for this elevation, first through his son M. Furius Camillus Arruntius, *cos.* 32 CE, later, as

Scribonianus, the rebel against Claudius in 42 CE, and then through his star-gazing grandson, Camillus Scribonianus, exiled in 52 CE.

51 One M'. Curius does figure among the *familiares* of Cicero; and the leaky Catilinarian Q. Curius was emphatically *natus haud obscuro loco* ('born to no obscure station', Sall. *Cat.* 23. 1)

52 Propertius sets an Ennian riddle: his dream-work swig from Ennius' cup inspired from one (or more) of the poets Ennius, Propertius, Propertius-as-Ennius and/or *vice versa*, the *Kataloggedicht* (catalogue poem) summarized in Prop. 3. 3. 7ff., beginning with (*et cecini<t?>*) *Curios fratres et Horatia pila*, 'and he/I sang of the Curii and the spears of the Horatii'. The very next item *appears* to condense dream-thoughts of *Aemilia tropaea* ('trophies of Aemilius') that belong to Paullus' triumph, two years *after* we believe that Ennius started to sleep the sleep of the just, so displacements are on the cards (Butrica [1983], Kierdorf [1994]): nowhere else do extant Horatii battle against triple *Curii*. Satirists liked to taunt metrically infelicitous names, which denied the chance for fame (cf. Gowers [1993] 63 n. 26).

53 On the **Scipiadic** fight with metrics, see Austin on Virg. *Aen.* 6. 842f. : Ovid commits his dactylic *Scipio* at *Ars* 3. 409f., *Ennius emeruit. . . contiguus poni, Scipio magne, tibi* ('E. earned the right to be set by your side, great Scipio'), where the dactyl *Ennius* equals the cut down to size *Scipio* in his next line (both:– ∪∪). Ennius made Scipio famous, but *not* by foreshortening his name-fame. Litchfield (1914) 50 points out how Curius' and Fabricius' prosaic mate *Coruncanius* (∪ - - ∪ -*us*) misses out in poetry (restricted to the vocative and genitive in hexameters).

54 Enter Scipio Africanus in triumph, *ipse adstans curru. . .* ('the man himself, stood up in his chariot', Sil. *Pun.* 17. 645).

55 Cf. *TLL* v. 1. 1205. 18, *de effigie ex parte dimidia expressa* (= of an effigy represented half-way). At Mart. 11. 18. 22, *dimidio. . . Priapo* ('half a Priapus') is a half-cocked castration-joke.

56 So Fredericks (1971) 115. We have seen that *imagines* are all about magnification of *fama* through *nomen* (Every encomiast's problem: Ov. *Ex Pont.* 4. 3. 41, *quid fuerat Magno maius?*, 'What had there been that was greater than Pompey the Great?')—from Pompeius Magnus to Fabius Maximus, Africanus Maior *vs.* Cato Maior—and indeed every

cos. maior (senior of the pair of consuls). So Lucan 6. 789f., *maior Karthaginis hostis, l. . . maeret Cato fata nepotis* ('the greater foe of Carthage,. . . Cato mourns the deathstiny of his descendant') both puts Cato Maior before Scipio Maior and compares the Catones Maior and Minor with Scipio Maior and Metellus Pius Scipio.

57 Ovid includes the torque of T. Manlius *Torquatus* with Valerius' *coruus* along with the properly triumphal and kindred *nomina: Africa*-nus, *Isaur*-icus, *Cret*-icus, *Numid*-icus, *Numantin*-us, with [Messalla] < *Messana*; then prince *Drusus* '*Germani*-cus'; [Pompeius] *Magn*-us and [Caesar] *nomine maior*; *Fabi*-us *Maxim*-us. All this as 'build-up' to the ultimate name, '*August-us*' (< *augustus*, 'holy', and < *augurium*, and < *augere*, 'augmented' with these name-fame-story-images, + < *auspicia*, Ov. *Fast.* 1. 590–616, see below, pp. 126–8). *Corvinus* is among Manilius' heroes ascended to their astral ring of fire (*Astron.* 1. 782f.). Silius has his soothsayer Corvinus croak nevermore, with raven for crest (*Pun.* 5. 78f., cf. vv. 77, 121f.).

58 Gell. *Noct. Att.* 9. 11. 10.

59 Cf. Syme (1986) 200–16, at 216, 'the direct line ended under Nero', with *stemma* at Table IX: Corvinus *cos.* 58 CE, and Taurus Statilius Corvinus, another grandson, *cos.* 45 CE and Claudian conspirator.

60 McCartney (1912) 29.

61 Unless apes have shoulders. Juvenal also gives the name the bird at 1. 108, *custodit in agro l. . . Coruinus ouis* ('on the farm, watching sheep is Raveny').

62 Courtney *ad loc.*

63 *Galba* is blessed with four mysterious derivations by Suet. *Galb.* 3: *galbanum, galbeus* (?), *galba*—a small grub, the ash-borer, so = 'thin' (I expect *they* have 'neither ears nor nose'), or from Gallic **Kalb*, so = 'fatso' (Corvinus *fought* Gauls. . .).

64 Cf. Murison on Suet. *Galb.* 31–2, with *stemma* at 174, Appendix B.

65 Cf. Suet. *Galb.* 2f., Plut. *Galb.* 3, Tac. *Hist.* 2. 76. 2. The effective pedigree, that led to the purple, was through his step-mother, a distant cousin of Livia Augusta: Galba was through testamentary adoption the *cos.* 33 CE *L. Livius Ocella Sulpicius Galba.* Silius' Galba leads Etruria, boasting the Minos descent (*Pun.* 8. 469ff., *magno. . . nomine*: in charge

of fraternal Umbria is *his* pretty boy Piso, at 463ff. ; foreshadowing of the Emperor at 10. 194–201, *Galba*. . . *occidit, immoriens magnis non prosperus ausis* ['Galba perished, dying on a great adventure, dogged by misfortune']).

66   Esp. Plut. *Galb.* 28. 3, *panta tropon aikisamenoi kai kathubrisantes* ('disfiguring and outraging it in every way').

67   Suet. *Galb.* 21. 1, *adunco naso*, shown off on his *sestertius* (a coin) from Rome of 68 CE (Kleiner [1992] 168, *fig.* 135). His *ears*—on coins at least—*are* on the diminutive side (*auri-culis*, 'earlets').

68   This is A. E. Housman's satirically back-handed compliment for this 'pretty smart & superior interpolation', *ad loc.* (*paulo scitius*). His own surgery, / *pontifices posse ac* . . . ('that priests can. . .') is dull indeed (but *would* link, as we shall see, with *equitum. . . magistros*, to *Lepidis*). His notion that neither proper name nor *any* word in the singular is wanted here does not do justice to the concatenation between vv. 1–5, 6–9, 9–12, and 13–18, with their characteristic blend of *variatio* with development of the argumentation. The *point*, anyhow, is sustained grammatical-conceptual play *between* singularity and plurality: **F a b r i c i u m** takes up 'an expanse of writing/painting-space', just as all the '*magg. eq. + dict.*' require 'lots and lots of branches' (*capaci* :: *multa*; cf. Juv. 1. 63, *ceras implere capaces*, 'fill expansive wax-tablets'). In terms of the social mix of names, *Aemilianos et Curios* yokes adoptive milords to plebeian hero(es), *cognomen* to *nomen*: **Coruinum** *et* **Galbam** pairs two patricians, *agnomen* and *cognomen*; *Fabricium*. . . *Lepidis* as a team would spell a second plebeian *nomen* + patrician *cognomen*; but the next limb has only a triumphal *agnomen*; and the last pairs an *agnomen* and *nomen* from the same *gens*. Considerations proliferate, taking us into the ramifying domain of stemmata.

69   This comes after the stories of Brutus the *Liberator*, and of a Cassius who was executioner of a revolutionary. Scaurus, the coward's father, and Fulvius, spawner of a Catilinarian, follow.

70   Cf. (e. g.) Mart. 9. 28. 4, 11. 16. 6, Serv. *Aen.* 6. 839, *Pyrrhum*. . . *Curius et Fabricius uicerunt* ('C. and F. won the original Pyrrhic victory'), Powell on Cic. *De Sen.* 55.

71   Very likely Horace is the inspiration of the MSS's *Fabricium*; but this

works for Juvenal at least as well as for any mediaeval scribe or Renaissance scholar.

72   Cf. West (1993) 291, 'In this context there may be a suggestion that he appears in the garb of a *faber*, a workman, to demonstrate that his strength was derived from his incorruptibility'.

73   The famous **Fabrician** bridge was actually built by the *curator uiarum* L. Fabricius in 62. At Juv. 4. 129f., the Domitianic 'informer' A. *Fabricius* Veiiento (*cos*. III) wants at once to *saw up* the great fish (*conciditur?*).

74   Cf. *auriculis nasoque carentem* / ↔ *tabula iactare capaci* /, vv. 5–6.

75   Serv. *Aen*. 1. 730 (cf. Cic. *In Pis*. 1, *commendatio fumosarum imaginum*). Preparing for the 'release' of / *tota*. . . / *atria*, vv. 19f. Can we [dare] bracket out vv. 6–8? As we shall see, this would spoil the Vitruvian symmetry of the architecture of this *exordium*, with '18 lines on either side' of the 'solemn statement' at vv. 19–20 (Braund [1988] 70).

76   Vitruvius advises that *imagines* should be set up on high together with their trappings' (*De Arch*. 6. 3. 6, *alte cum suis ornamentis. . . sint constitutae*).

77   Syme (1986) 104–40. *Stemmata*: *ib*. Tables IV, V, VIII, *RE*. 1. 562 (starting from the post-Sullan Lepidus, *cos*. 78). There were also consular Manii and Quinti Lepidi a-plenty; even a Mamercus. For Drusilla's Lepidus, see Lindsay on Suet. *Gai*. 24. 3, Syme (1986) 179.

78   Arch Manilius (*Astron*. 1. 796) may asterize / *Aemiliae*. . . *domus proceres* ('leaders of the house of Aemilii') after his palace-watcher courtier's *Claudi magna propago,* / (v. 795, 'great offshoot of Claudius'), so as to include together the family amalgam of the Aemilii Lepidi Paulli: in 43 L. Paulus (*cos*. 50) had his brother M. Lepidus (the future *IIIuir*) declared *hostis*. Lepidus' homonymous son was executed to bless Actium; Paulus' son L. Aemilius Lepidus Paullus, *aka* Paullus Aemilius Lepidus (*cos*. *suff*. 34) completed his father's *Basilica Aemilia*, or *porticus Paulli*: *his* sons were M. Lepidus (*cos*. 6 CE), *capax imperii* ('a possible Emperor'), whose daughter married Germanicus' son Drusus, and L. Paullus (*cos*. 1 CE), who married Julia Minor, but lost his head; meanwhile, M'. Lepidus (*cos*. 11 CE) earned respect from Augus-

tus, Tiberius—and Tacitus. Plenty of fatal ironies here for the poet of fatalism.

79 Cf. Cicero's cavillation, '[Junia], sister to your friend [Brutus], brute enough to exploit this, and wife of that charmer [**Lepidus**], charming enough to put up with all this with such *sang froid*.' (*Ad Att.* 6. 1. 25: [*Iuniae*] *sororis amici tui, hominis bruti* [*Bruti*], *qui hoc utatur, et* <*uxoris illius lepidi* [*Lepidi*], *qui haec tam neglegenter ferat*).

80 Cunctator holds any *Punica* up long enough to deny himself a place in Elysium there. Silius' roll-call must end ominously with a Lethaean *pre-view* of Caesar and Pompey (paired with just the pair Marius and Sulla. . .): no Virgilian tail-piece of Fabii or Marcelli at *this* (dramatic) date.

81 **Fabius** *Cunctator* successfully protracts Silius' epic into a seventeenth book: he holds up Hannibal until Scipio can overcome *him* and become Africanus (Fabius = *mora*, 'delay', *Pun.* 8. 33. By introducing Fabius, Silius without delay ends *Pun.* 1, with *nec. . . morentur.* //, v. 693; 'nor do they delay'); textual entry of *Cunctator* signals digression, esp. at 6. 639, *cunctando* (+ *Campania*'s campaigns of sloth), then ecphrasis from 658–716 (= from the end of the book/session); 7. 126, *sollers cunctandi* ('with a flair for delaying') Bacchus' and Falernus' the-oxeny/Champagne conviviality from 162–211. From *Pun.* 7. 20 on, *noua nomina lecto* / *dictatore vigent*, where Hannibal 'is impressed to read what for him is a strange barbarism' and 'the election of a dictator brings maximal reinforcement to the front/new names to the front: fresh blood', Fabius regularly appears as *dictator*, e. g. still remembered by Hannibal at 12. 501, *Fabius Fabiique magister*.

82 The clan made sure to be mystified by a string of etymologies, 'Human Beans' (< *faba*-growers, Plin. *Nat. Hist.* 18. 10), 'Last-Ditchers' (< *Fodius* < *fodio*, Plut. *Fab.* 1. 2), 'The Pits' (< *Fouius* < *fovea*, Paul. Fest. 87), and a fist of strange *cognomina* (*Buteones*, 'Hawks', *Dossuones*, 'Hunchbacks', *Gurgites*, 'Gluttons', *Labeones*, 'Rubber Lips', *Pictores*, 'Whitewashers'. . .). Through Fabius Pictor, they more or less invented Roman history—as word-painting ecphrasis. Nepos wrote a book on the clan (*Att.* 18. 4).

83 Syme (1986) 77, 418; cf. Ov. *Ex Pont.* 3. 3. 99f., Sil. *Pun.* 6. 627–36.

Herculeus and *Tirynthius* are Fabian standing epicthets in *Punica*. The *triumphator* removed a colossal Hercules from Tarentum to the Capitol, where it lasted past Pliny's day (*Nat. Hist.* 34. 40).

84 Cf. Ov. *Fast.* 2. 195–452, dominated by cunctation: vv. 195–242 tell of the 306 Fabii against Veii, closed with *cunctando*; the next tale *non faciet longas. . . moras. . . '. . . ne quid. . . moretur.., . . . tarda. . . mora,. . . morae* (vv. 248, 249, 256, 259); then vv. 267–452 overhaul the *Luperci*, with the *Fabii* emerging, after all this text, at vv. 375, 377, as its centre-piece (vv. 365–80). On this subject, I help myself to the generous insights of Harries (1991).

85 Plut. *Fab.* 1. 2. Son of a Fabius Ambustus and sometimes known as *Rullus*, the form of his usual name *Rullianus* suggests he has been adopted from the Rullus family.

86 *Stemma* for Fabii Maximi at Syme (1986) Table XXVII, *RE.* 6. 1778.

87 Fragment from Rome, supplemented by the Arezzo *elogium* (Degrassi, [1937] 21, no. 14 + 60f., no. 80).

88 Syme (1986) 403; Juv. *Sat.* 7. 95. Paulus became schismatic Horace's (first) figurehead for *Odes* 4, as the 'Callimachean' oxymoron on legs *Paulus* ↔ *Maximus*, 'Shorty the Man Mountain', that greatest/modest collection of ditties for Venus the sex-kitten-*cum*-epic matriarch of the Roman race (4. 1. 10f-.15. 32; the second is *Iulus* ↔ *Antonius*, 4. 2. 2, 26).

89 Syme (1986) 417f.

90 Syme (1986) 415.

91 Syme (1986) 418f.

92 Seneca adds *Cunctator* to *Allobrogicus* as Persicus' favourite forebears (*De. Ben.* 4. 30. 2). He forbears to extend the catechism.

93 Cf. Syme (1986) 282f., 'Aemilii, Fabii, and Valerii renovated their splendour, through favour of Caesar Augustus, but went out before the dynasty ended. The last Aemilius Lepidus perished in a conspiracy, no Fabius held the *fasces* after Persicus. . ., no Valerius Messalla after the impoverished colleague of Nero. . . . Even the Lentuli. . . show no consul after the year 68.'

94 Deplored by Sen. *De Ben.* 4. 30. 2.

95 Cic. *Tusc. Disp.* 1. 81; Val. Max. 3. 5. 2: second, in the chapter *Qui a*

Parentibus Claris Degenerauerunt ('Those who degenerated from acclaimed parents'), to. . . the son of Scipio Africanus Maior. . . ; 6. 9. 4.

96 Fest. 245; Ps-. Quint. *Decl.* 3. 17; Val. Max. 6. 1. 5, *RE.* 6. 1797. 47ff.

97 Macrob. *Sat.* 3. 13. 6; cf. Juv. *Sat.* 6. 266.

98 Livy is here adorning Claudius Quadrigarius' version *ap.* Gell. *Noct. Att.* 2. 2. 13.

99 Sil. *Pun.* 15. 322f., *postremus in armis / ductoris titulus cauti* ('the final citation in combat of the cagey general').

100 *Cunctator's laudatio funebris* (funeral speech) for his son was one of the earliest to survive into Roman libraries. He had the sense (of poetic history) to die himself in 203, as Hannibal quit Italy, but before he could (have to) vote Scipio the 'new name' *Africanus*.

101 Cic. *De Sen.* 12, cf. Sil. *Pun.* 7. 691–704, Cato a seventeen-year-old head-hunter in the *dictator* Fabius' rescue of Minucius, 10. 14f. at Cannae.

102 Try Juv. *Sat.* 8. 191, where members of the clan act on the stage (cf. Dio. *Hist.* 61. 17).

103 Ov. *Fast.* 2. 195–242: note *una domus, una dies. . . una dies, unus. . . relictus erat* ('one clan, one day, one day, one of them was left').

104 Ov. *Fast.* 2. 225: Harries (1991) 154f. explains how Ovid signals 'Callimachean' inverse proportionality between the scale of his treatment of the Fabii and their greatness; and enjoys Ovid's mimetically breakneck re-presentation of their dashing *uirtus*.

105 In the *Culex*, the catalogue in honour of the heroic gnat (cued by *heroes. . . omnes, / omnes. . . magni*, vv. 359f., 'all the heroes, all, the great') therefore begins from *Fabii Deciique*, with *Horatia uirtus* (Horatii Brothers *vs.* Curiatii, or Horatius at the Bridge?) inserted before *Camill<us /*, where Virgil had and has—fictionally, 'will have'—*Decios Marios magnosque Camillos / (Georg.* 2. 169: for *Decios Mures)* and *Decios Drusosque. . . Torquatum. . . Camillum / (Aen.* 6. 824f.); *Curtius* and *Mucius Scaeuola* continue the theme (*Culex* vv. 361, 362–6: then [through *incuria?*] *Curius*, and finally another moth to the flame of devotion, a certain ²*Flaminius*², v. 368). Lucan and Silius have no Fabius in their 'roll-calls'.

106 Virg. *Aen.* 8. 271f.

107 Perverse stylist, anti-antiquarian pedant, and satirically abusive, Tacitus alters the Ara Maxima to *magna ara* in his potted history of the city-limits— and when it is burnt down in Nero's Fire (*Ann.* 12. 24. 1, 15. 41. 1): Juvenal humbles the Altar for a similar hotch-potch of motives; the biggest of them all, to maximize the Fabii. *Allobrogicis et magna. . . ara* may also fool the reader into thoughts of the altar of Rome and Augustus planted at Lugdunum (age-old rival of Allobrogian Vienne) before we reach *Herculeo Fabius* in v. 14?

108 Virgil's Evander warned Aeneas 'You are now entering where Hercules stooped after conquering: dare to scorn wealth, mould yourself to match divine dignity' (*Aen.* 8. 362–4).

109 Sil. *Pun.* 6. 613–15, cf. 7. 566f., *expers irarum senior* ('the old head, free from tides of wrath') etc.

110 Sil. *Pun.* 6. 616. Cf. Cic. *De Sen.* 10, Plut. *Fab.* 1. 3.

111 So Plin. *Nat. Hist.* 3. 134, *ex comitatu Herculis. . . eiusdem exercitus et Graios fuisse Graiarum Alpium incolas praestantesque genere Euganeos, inde tracto nomine* ('from the entourage of Hercules. . . in the same army there were also 'Graii', the inhabitants of the Graian Alps, and those oustanding in their pedigree, the **Euganei**, their name deriving from that fact').

112 E. g. Sil. *Pun.* 7. 151f. (Hannibal), *inuentum, dum se cohibet, terimurque sedendo, / uincendi genus* ('A category of conquest has been devised, where he reins himself in and we get worn down as we sit there'). Stonewall Fabius was Hannibal's pumice: 'with his endurance he softened up Hannibal, who crowed as boys will' (Cic. *De Sen.* 10, *Hannibalem iuueniliter exsultantem patientia sua molliebat*). Hence the degenerate scion *must* be *mollior*.

113 Plut. *Fab.* 1. 3. Elogia do not descend to such life in the raw as **Ouicula**, **Verrucosus** or even **Cunctator**.

114 Perhaps with catachrestic (derogatory) connotations of 'dissoluteness', as Courtney hazards.

115 A self-deleting phrase, for in law 'the purchase of poison makes no contract at law' (Gaius *Dig.* 18. 1. 35. 2, *ueneni mali non contrahi emptionem* — except. . . for medicinal purposes).

116 E.g. Tac. *Ann.* 11. 35. 2, 'He ordered the house opened up, and first

150

he pointed out in the hall the likeness of Silius *père*, decreed for destruction by the senate' (*patefieri domum. . . iubet. ac primum in uestibulo effigiem patris Silii consulto senatus abolitam demonstrat*). Cf. Nadeau (1985) for similar explication of Juvenal's manifold imagery in vv. 17f.

117 Contrast v. 55, *tua uiuit imago* ('your image lives').

118 With *sola. . . atque unica*, v. 20, cf. (e. g.) Ov. *Fast.* 2. 240, *unus*, annexed to Cremera from Ennius' elogium of *Cunctator* at 242; or Sil. *Pun.* 7. 1, *trepidis Fabius spes unica rebus* ('**Fabius**, the only hope in a crisis').

119 Cf. Marius in Sall. *Bell. Iug.* 85. 17, *ex **uirtute** nobilitas coepit* ('Nobility started from courage').

120 For discussion of *uirtus* by Lucilius and later satirists, cf. Raschke (1990).

121 Cf. Edwards (1993) *passim*.

122 Anyone can play, for this *is* the Roman game: *si nobiles iuuenes dignum aliquid. . . faciant...* ('if noble youths should do something worthy. . .', Plin. *Epp.* 5. 17. 1, with Sherwin-White, 'Syme. . . waxes most indignant at Pliny's condescension.').

123 As we noticed above, cf. Braund (1988) 70.

124 See the 'themes' picked out in Chapter 10 above. The phrasing of the second commandment, *maiorum. . . tuorum /*, v. 22, will haunt the poem, cf. vv. 3, 64, (133,) 146, 227, 274 and 74, 274.

125 Cf. *ouanti / ~ Osiri /*, vv. 28f. With *contingis*, v. 28, cf. *contingere*, v. 7. Chiasmus makes the ablatival constructions pun in reading: *indignus genere et praeclaro nomine. . . → indignus genere ↔ praeclaro nomine. . . insignis*.

126 Juvenal serves up sickness in labials: *scabie. . . leuibus. . . lambentibus. . . lucernae* (vv. 34f.).

127 See Salway (1994) 130, 'The Eclipse of the *Praenomen*', Syme (1958) 173–5, (1986) 75f. : *Faustus Sulla, Potitus Valerius Messalla. . .* 'Transferences then became exorbitant'. Wiseman (1970), esp. 211f., notes how some Late Republicans used 'both the traditional style and the transferred *cognomen*', as L. Valerius Potitus Messalla *or* Potitus Valerius Messalla, others were constant, as **Cossus** Cornelius Lentulus.

128 *Paulus* (Little) typifies *maiores* (The Greater Ones, Ancestors) thanks

to a very old pun by reversal, as in Sil. *Pun.* 8. 298, *maxima. . . Paule*, 306, *quantum. . . Paule*, 10. 305–8, *hic finis Paulo. iacet altum pectus et ingens / dextera, quem soli. . . / aequares forsan Fabio*[*sc. Maximo*] *. . . inter sidera nomen* ('Such was Paulus' end. Fallen that lofty heart and vast right hand, a man whom you could equate, maybe, to Fabius. A famous name to join the stars.'). The Aemilii claimed descent, via Amulius and Assaracus, from Jupiter (*ib.* 8. 293–7); M. Paullus was *cos.* 302 and *mag. eq.* of the *dictator* Q. Fabius Maximus in 301; M. Paullus was *cos.* 255 and *triumphator* 254; L. Paullus (*cos.* 219, *triumphator ex Illyricis*) died a hero at Cannae (as *cos.* II), and so became the latest arrival in Silius' roll-call: Scipio's father-in-law (*Pun.* 13. 706). We saw that L. Paullus Macedonicus (*coss.* 182, 168, *triumphator* II, *de Liguribus, de Macedonicis*), who is an 'enigma' in Virgil's roll-call (*Aen.* 6. 838–40), died the most famous of fathers, but as the self-doomed last of the Paulli (Liv. *A. U. C.* 45. 40. 7–42. 1, Polyb. *Hist.* 34. 14. 2). The story must start again, we saw, from the Caesarian L. Paullus, *cos.* 50 and brother of Lepidus (Syme [1986] 106, '"Paullus" for *cognomen* by a bold and urbane usurpation').

129 Virg. *Aen.* 6. 841: *Augustus* did not 'leave him to silence', since he had **Cossus'** inscribed Veientine *spolia* re-decorated in the cosseted Temple of Jupiter Feretrius (Liv. *A. U. C.* 4. 20. 5f.); Manilius pairs him with **Marcellus**, for their *spolia* (*Astron.* 1.788). Fifth and fourth-century Cornelii Cossi proliferated. Of the Augustan general's sons, Cossus was *cos. ord. maior* 25 CE and Cn. Lentulus Gaetulicus *cos. ord. maior* 26 CE; the latter was executed for conspiracy by Gaius in 39 CE, one of his sons was *cos. suff.* in 55 CE, and Cossus Cornelius Lentulus was *cos.* 60 CE. (On Juvenal's *Cossi*, cf. LaFleur [1972].)

130 Cf. Woodman on Vell. 2. 116. 2.

131 Suet. *Tib.* 3.

132 Virgil pairs **Decios Drusosque procul**, then **Torquatum** ('snapped' as *Torquatus Imperiosus* executing *his* insubordinate son) *et. . . Camillum* (*Aen.* 6. 824f.). **Decii** force their neighbours' records as Father-Son emulation under our noses: we may try to think pure, 'far-off', thoughts of M. Livius Salinator (*coss.* 219, 207), victor over Hasdrubal in 207 (an 'honorary' Drusus, cf. Hor. *Carm.* 4. 4. 37ff., Manil. *Astron.* 1. 791,

Liuius. . . socio. . . Nerone, 'L. with Nero for mate'); and of M. Livius Drusus (*tr. pl.* 122, *cos.* 112), senatorial bulwark against C. Gracchus. But it is not going to be possible to obliviate his son M. Livius Drusus, *tr. pl.* 91, whose ructions earn the name dejection to join Lucan's Sinners: *popularia nomina, Drusos, / legibus immodicos* ('revolutionary names, the Drusi, using laws to fashion excess', *Bell. Ciu.* 6. 795f.). For Libo Drusus, cf. Syme (1986) 256f. ; *stemmata, ib.* Tables XIV, XV, XIX.

133 The reference of *hos* and *illi* eludes decision: most commentators rule that both signify *mores* (not Ferguson: 'these people, *not* mores'). Gnilka (1969) 93f., ousts *ante* + *pone,* v. 22, as = 'prefer', in favour of 'set up in front of'. But if you mean to climb right inside this poem, it is important to work this imagery *of* imagery hard: cf. other phrases in the poem with apparent spatial force: *fuga ante alios et primus. . . Coryphaei posteritas,* vv. 61f., *praeferre,* vv. 83, 139, 212, *post omnia,* v. 97, *statuamque parentis / ante,* vv. 144f., *ante altaria,* v. 156, *ante pedes. . . pone,* v. 228.

134 *praecedant. . . uirgas* adds its own inside-out touch of reversal, since lictors 'carried their symbolic bundles of rods in front' of them, *and* carried themselves ahead of their consul; but the symbolic lictors symbolize the consul's *imperium,* as do the *fasces,* so this is a conceptual knot of cultural power. *Multi*valence in *uirgas* is hard to deny after the play in *multa. . . uirga,* v. 7.

135 D. Iunius **Silanus Gaetulicus** was a Salian priest in 63 CE: a grandson of the *cos.* of 1 BCE given out to adoption? Or 'advertisement of maternal ascendance by the *cognomen*'? (Syme [1986] 194, Table XIII: with a son M. Silanus Lutatius Catulus).

136 Juvenal leaves *seu tu /* (v. 26) to dangle at the end of the verse. Maybe to threaten an insult?

137 With *quocumque* cf. v. 60, *quocumque. alio* signals the blur in *Gaetulicus-Silanus* (one family, or two?); there is no call to emend and spoil v. 40, *alto.*

138 With *generosus,* v. 30, cf. *generosa → equum,* vv. 57f., *generosi* (*Neronis*), v. 224; of lions and elephants, cf. Beagon (1992) 149f. : Juvenal turns toward slaves (vv. 32–4), then *dogs* (vv. 34–7).

139 . . . *hunc qui* / (v. 30) dangles menacingly at the end of the verse.

140 These names are chosen *exempli gratia*, by initial: *cauebis. . . Creticus. . . Camerinus* (vv. 37f.): *si quid. . .. est. . . in terris* (vv. 36f.) ushers in the geographical sweep in the names. For Coruncanius as from the Latin town **Camerium**, not the usual Tusculum, because Claudius knew he was there before the town's destruction, cf. Tac. *Ann.* 11. 24. 1 (with Syme [1958A] Vol. II, 710 n. 4). For early *Camerini*, cf. Juv. *Sat.* 7. 90, Ser. Sulpicii Camerini, *cos.* 500; *cos.* 461; *cos.* 393; Q. Sulpicii Camerini *cos.* 434; *mil. tr.* 402. 'No consul since 345 B.C.' (Syme [1986] 98): Augustan revival, Q. Sulpicius Camerinus, *cos.* 9 CE; then Q. Sulpicius Camerinus Peticus, *cos. suff.* 46 CE, 'the last consul of the patrician Sulpicii', Syme (1986) 280 n. 70. Cf. *ib.* 75, 'Towns or villages of old Latium now come to life in *cognomina*. . . A Sulpicius emerges as Camerinus.'

Q. Caecilius Metellus (*cos.* 69) conquered Crete and was hailed *imperator* in 67; he triumphed and was awarded the title *Creticus* in 62 (Sall. *Hist.* 2. 45): thus *cos.* 7 CE was Q. Caecilius Metellus Creticus, and *his* son was Creticus Iunius Silanus (Syme [1986] 196, 253, Table XVIII, 'The Last Metelli'). On the other hand, M. Antonius Creticus, 'the son of a famous father and the father of a famous son', died on Crete as *propr.* 74–71, so the title could not be without irony, however far short of an insult to his memory it might fall (Linderski [1990], Plut. *Ant.* 1, Appian. *Sicil.* 6). Ovid includes Crete on his list: **Cretum domitas testificatur** opes (*Fast.* 1. 594).

141 For a toned down version cf. Hor. *Serm.* 1. 3. 38–75, esp. 56–8, *probus quis* / *nobiscum uiuit, multum demissus homo: illi* / *tardo cognomen, pingui damus* ('Some good person in our company, a real downer of a guy: we give him the tag of "slowcoach", or "plump"'. Cf. Brown *ad loc.* for erotic euphemisms: to catalogue them is to undo and *reverse* their signification). Juvenal's *Europen*, v. 34, alludes to this topic, and with black → white in v. 33, cf. Lucr. *De Rer. Nat.* 4. 160, *nigra melichrus est* ('a black girl is "honey"', Ov. *Ars* 2. 657f., *fusca uocatur*, / *nigrior*, 'a jet black girl is called "dusky"').

142 vv. 11, 13, 26, 38; 21. Cf. Braund (1988) 65f. for the (misguided)

dispute over the honorific/derogatory epithet in *Ciceronem Allobroga*, 7. 214.

143 In the Forum Augustum, as we saw: cf. the decoction of Manil. *Astron.* 1. 783, *qui gestat in alite Phoebum* ('who bears Apollo in bird-form').

144 vv. 9, 21, 40, 93, 96 *bis*, 105, 106, 151, 182, 187, 222, 244, 264. Various *nomina* carry their stories, too: *Curii, Fabricius, Fabius, Mucius* (vv. 4, 6, 14, 264). Even the more opaque can play: *Galba, Cossus, Silanus...* (vv. 5, 21, 27).

145 I follow Clausen's Oxford Text, with the deletions he accepts, plus vv. 48b-49a, for which cf. n. 148 below. On v. 220, *Orestes / Oresten*, see Bartsch (1994) 50.

146 A good pupil would know the august genealogy from Laurentine Picus pecked out in Virg. *Aen.* 7. 170–91, esp. *ueterum effigies ex ordine auorum / antiqua e cedro...,... imago / uestibulo astabant*, 'likenesses of the ancient forefathers made of venerable cedar... and... *imago* stood to in the hallway', vv. 177–8.

147 *discinxerit Afros /*, 120 < Virg. *Aen.* 8. 724, *discinctos... Afros /*.

148 I accept the deletion of *praestare Neronem / securum ualet haec aetas*, vv. 170f., advocated by Nisbet (1962) 236.

149 Venus brings *Aeneas* precisely *Volcaniaque arma*, in the same metrical *sedes*, at *Aen.* 8. 535 (cf. *arma... Volcania*, 12. 739).

150 The 'generalizing plural' *Volesos* makes the singular *Brutum* reverberate with tension. The first Volesus came to Rome with Titus Tatius; heading the *Fasti Consulares* for ever was P. Valerius *Publicola ingentis Volesi Spartana propago* ('Publicola the Spartan offshoot of mighty Volesus', Sil. *Pun.* 2. 8–10). The *cognomen Volesus* was revived by Augustan Valerii: L. Valerius Pot. f. Messalla Volesus (*cos.* 5 CE, Syme (1986) Table X).

151 *This* Marius did *not* defeat and capture Colonel Jugurtha: Marius Priscus, condemned for maladministration in 100 CE (see Courtney on 1. 49).

152 If we keep the reference to **Nero** in v. 170, this must, but cannot, be Plautius **Lateranus**, removed from the senate in 48 CE, restored in Nero's honeymoon year of 55 CE, but eliminated in the Pisonian reprisals of 65 CE as *cos. des.* (Cf. 10. 17). This would be a 'bad historical mistake'

155

(Courtney): bad enough for a great satirist. T. Sextius Lateranus, *cos.* 94 CE, is (otherwise) but a name. *Lateranus* is a 'Brickie' (Arnob. *Adv. Nat.* 4. 6, *deus est focorum* ['god of hearths']), and as such belongs, perhaps, 'in a great inn' (Juv. *Sat.* 8. 172, *in magna. . . popina*), but the name can bespeak 'Loins' too (cf. Sil. *Pun.* 5. 229f., *amore /. . . in medios penetrauerat hostes* / ['L. had penetrated deep into the hearts of the enemy, through love'], with Juv. 8. 173–6, *cum. . . iacentem,* / *permixtum. . . / inter.* ['lying down. . . with, mixed up. . . amongst']).

153 For **Lentuli** and **Fabii**, etc., on Nero's stage, cf. Dio *Hist.* 61. 17. 4. See Syme (1986) 284–99 for the *gens,* and Tables XXI and XXII for 'The Last Lentuli'—to the end of the Julio-Claudians.

154 *Mamercus* is said to mean 'Mars' in Sabine and to have been an Oscan *praenomen* (paired with *Appius* by Sil. *Pun.* 5. 333ff.); a *cognomen* of the *gens Aemilia,* which claimed him for founder, the son of Pythagoras, or of Numa. *Mam.* Lepidus Livianus, Livius Drusus' brother, was *cos.* 77; the last Scaurus (we saw) was *Mam.* Aemilius Scaurus.

155 Virgil puts his *Gracchi genus* with the Scipios (*Aen.* 6. 842): we are bound (with Feeney [1986] 13) to think of two of Cornelia's twelve children, the tribune 'revolutionaries' Ti. and C. Gracchus—along with their celebrated father Ti. Gracchus (*cos.* 177, 163), and the Hannibalic casualty (*cos.* 215, 213: just arrived in Silius' *katabasis, Pun.* 13. 717). Silius plays with the so far untainted *stemma*: *Gracchorum proles, consul* (*Ti. Sempronius Longus*), *gens inclita. . . multusque in imagine claris* / *praefulgebat auus titulis bellique domique. . . degener haud Gracchis consul* ('the offspring of the Gracchi, a consul. . . and a famous clan, with many a forefather's *imago* shining bright with their citations in battle and at home. . ., no way degenerating from the Gracchi', 4. 495–7, 515). Lucan firmly demotes to the Sinners his *ausos. . . immania Gracchos* / ('Gracchi, those gross adventurers', *Bell. Ciu.* 6. 796, in a rhyme with the *Drusos* / of v. 795). 'No consular Sempronii Gracchi followed on the two ambitious tribunes' (Syme [1986] 16).

156 Nero's revival of his natural fathering by L. Domitius Ahenobarbus is brought to our attention at v. 228, *Domiti* (Cf. esp. Tac. *Ann.* 13. 10).

157 Cicero appears in Manil. *Astron.* 1. 794f., *censu Tullius oris* / *emeruit fasces* ('Tully earned the *fasces* with his mouth's collateral'; cf. Juv. *Sat.*

8. 260, *fasces meruit?*). Lucan takes *Catilina* from Virgil's shield of Aeneas (*Aen.* 8. 668) and teams him with *Marii* and *Cethegi* for the Sinners' jail-break (*Bell. Ciu.* 6. 793f.). *Cethegus* fouled the name of M. Cornelius Cethegus (*cos.* 204), praised by Ennius and victor over Hannibal's brother Mago (Powell on Cic. *De Sen.* 50). 'For the ancient Sergii, the desperate ambition of Catilina had not availed', Syme (1986) 78, cf. Syme (1982) 67f.

158 As we saw, Virgil's Italy breeds *Decios Marios magnosque Camillos* / (*Georg.* 2. 169), but Anchises 'corrects' (weeds) his list to *Decios Drusosque. . . Camillum* / (*Aen.* 6. 824f.). Lucan puts his *Mariique* between *Catilina* and *Cethegi*, in the Sinners' sentence (*Bell. Ciu.* 6. 793–5). Silius enjoys using the name **Marius** (a friend of young Scipio), untainted at his dramatic date (*Pun.* 13. 231–3), but his Sibyl's flash into the future starts with *hic Marius. . . nec Sulla* before further decline to Virgil's pair of Pompey and Caesar (13. 853–67: Scipio is more interested in fast-forwarding Hannibal's end, vv. 868–93. Marius holds *longum imperium* but as *consul*; Sulla first seizes *imperium*, but resigns it, without successor. . .).

159 As we just saw, Virgil partners *Decios* with *Marios* or *Drusos*, forcing the reader to think over these other plurals: the Decii clone Son from Father as fax to original. So too Lucan leads off with *uidi Decios natumque patremque. . . Camillum* / *et Curios* (*Bell. Ciu.* 6. 785–7), *Culex* with *hic Fabii Deciique...* (v. 361). In Manilius, they share a verse, yet 'compete with each other, as well as the other contenders for astral fame', *certantes Decii uotis similesque triumphis* (*Astron.* 1. 789; cf. the plurals and singular in 4. 86f., *Decios. . . Camillos* /. . . *Catonem* /.).

160 Virg. *Aen.* 6. 814f. 'Servius is the only king to receive a lengthy obituary' from Livy (*A. U. C.* 1. 48. 8f.), Pomeroy (1988) 177 (on Marius, Fabius, Scipio Africanus, Cicero, *ib.* 178–80).

161 **Mucius** figures in the roll-call of *Culex*, soon after *Horatia uirtus* (vv. 365f., 361): Manilius calls the Horatii *Horatia proles*, and follows with the group *Scaeuola. . . Cloelia uirgo. . . Cocles* (*Astron.* 1. 778–81; cf. 4. 31–4, *Mucius. . . Horatius. . . uirgo. . . tresque. . . fratres*). Silius' Sibyl *ora docet uenientum et nomina pandit* ('teaches the faces of them as they approach and reveals their names'), then makes us 'see' and name

the blind Appius Claudius, and intuit the fame of 'one-eyed' *Cocles* (*Pun.* 13. 724–8). Virgil features on Aeneas' shield *Cocles / et. . . innaret Cloelia* (*Aen.* 8. 650f.).

162 The commentaries don't mention the quotation: *fascis. . . consulis imperium hic primus saeuasque securis / accipiet, natosque pater. . . / ad poenam pulchra pro libertate uocabit, / infelix, utcumque ferent ea facta minores. . ., Aen.* 6. 818–23 ~ *fasces. . . iuuenes ipsius consulis et quos / magnum aliquid dubia pro libertate deceret, / at illos uerbera iussis / adficiunt poenis et legum prima securis,* Juv. *Sat.* 8. 260–8. The satirist responds directly to the challenge in 6. 822: like Feeney (1986) 10f., I feel 'dubious' about the reception of this story of Republican fascism.

163 Cic. *De Fin.* 2. 61.

164 Liv. *A. U. C.* 1. 39–48.

165 *matronis lugendus,* 'for the matrons to mourn', v. 267: Liv. *A. U. C.* 2. 7. 4.

166 See Braund (1981). *I* think that *palma* fuses 'palm symbol of victory' and 'palms of a thousand applauding claps' because this puts the real victory literally in the hands of the *populus Romanus.* Horse-trading is a daft terrain for Juvenal to fight (vv. 57–67), since *The Pedigree* has paradigmatic purchase on the turf above all other scenarios.

167 Cf. Braund (1988) 71.

168 Tac. *Ann.* 6. 27. 1.

169 *per maternam originem pari ac Nero gradu a diuo Augusto... ; nobilitas per matrem ex Iulia familia,* Tac. *Ann.* 13. 19. 3, 14. 22. 2, 59. 6.

170 *CIL* 6. 16057.

171 Sen. *Contr.* 2 *Praef.* 5, Syme (1986) 173: cf. 354, 373 for the theory that he was Tiberius' teacher (with Syme [1982]). For the *stemma,* cf. Courtney on v. 39.

172 The politics of the Empire are therefore at once put into the book's window-sale: within this frame, oneiric silliness about the bad old days of the ancestors, and the worse ones of the more recent past, can never fail to be more than that.

173 For this invitation to think dirtier than the writer, cf. Augustin. *Civ. Dei* 4. 6.

174 On Naevolus, cf. Henderson (1989) 69f.

175 Cf. the famous frame of Callim. *Hymn* 2. See how Horace-Orpheus stills the elements (vv. 9f.); Jupiter brings all the seasons round (vv. 15f.): his winter storms will discontent the infidel other, not his sunny, vernal, jovial congregation (vv. 59f. : thunder, as Jove's chariot sky-quakes, v. 58, and lightning, *inimica. . . fulmina lucis* ['thunder*flashes* that persecute *clearings* in the dark groves'], vv. 59f., where *fulgeo*, 'flash', sparks against *lucus*, named as if *a non lucendo*, 'from not shedding light').

176 *secundo Caesare* both doubles for *augusto* (= *Augusto*) *Caesare diui filio*, and tells us that *this* Caesar successor *would* tolerate a superior (namely Jove), unlike Diuus Iulius, who precisely would not (see Lucan, *Bell. Ciu.* 1. 125f.).

177 *Numa Pompilius* becomes the Virgilian kenning, *legibus* ('laws', *Aen.* 6. 810: = *nomois*, cf. Serv. *ad* 808) + *Pompilius missus in imperium magnum* ('P.'s mission for greatness in command', v. 812; = *pompê* + quasi-diminutive suffix; add *sacra* ['holies'], v. 809, = *numen* ['holiness'] cf. Schol. Pers. *Sat.* 2. 59).

178 For recent treatment, see Brown (1991).

179 For their provocatively jangled evocations as good to think with, see Feeney (1986) 9ff. I shall be echoing many of the ideas in this seminal essay, as of the reactions to it in West (1993).

180 Contrast Manilius' note of precision, *Tarquinioque minus reges* to light *his* fiery roll-call ('the kings—minus Tarquin', *Astron.* 1. 778): *his* no-nonsense *Brutus* is [*Romae*] *a rege receptae / conditor* ('founder of Rome, vindicated from its king', v. 785f.). Luc. *Bell Ciu.* 6. 792f. specifies the 'first consul', the only good soul full of glee, because his namesake will soon 'deject *his* tyrant'; but Catiline & crew follow at once, making a break for de-segregation in Hades (vv. 793ff.).

181 Cf. Sil. *Pun.* 13. 721f., *meritum saeua Brutum immortale securi / nomen* ('Brutus who earned his eternal name and fame with his brutal axe').

182 Manil. *Astron.* 1. 797f. makes Stoic *Cato fortunae uictor* ('conqueror of Fortune'), so that his own rationalist mockery of 'chance' can chime in with *fictorque sub armis / miles Agrippa suae* ('fabricator of his Fortune under arms, soldier Agrippa', *ib.*)

183 Thus Manil. *Astron.* 1. 784f., *Ioue qui meruit caelum Romamque*

Camillus / *seruando posuit* ('Camillus who earned heaven from Jove and "built" Rome in preserving it').

184 Posidonius (*ap.* Plut. *Marcell.* 1. 1) claimed that 'He was first named **Marcellus**, i.e. martial' (*klêthênai prôton Markellon, hoper estin areion*); cf. Sil. *Pun.* 11. 99–101, 12. 278f., *Martis adaequant* / *Marcellum decori* ('they liken M. to the grace of Mars'), 420f., *Marcello* = *pugna* ('battle'), 15. 337f., *moles illa uiri, calidoque habitata Gradiuo* / *pectora* ('that *massif* of a man, a heart where white-hot Mars made his home'). *Marcellus* was used by very many *gentes*, but the plebeian Claudii Marcelli monopolized its fame. *How* ironic is Juv. *Sat.* 2. 145, *generosior. . . Marcellis* ('higher-born than the Marcelli').

185 Marcellus' acme was included within *Cunctator*'s in Enn. *Ann.* 8, as it is in Silius (*Pun.* 12. 256–15. 385). In *Pun.* 14, his still live Sicilian conquests immediately follow the Scipionic roll-call of heroic dead to end 13: as if Virgil (will have) made art follow life by tacking him onto *his* parade.

186 Sall. *Bell. Cat.* 25. 4–10. Last of the family was Mam. Aemilius **Scaurus**, . *cos.* 21 CE, *insignis nobilitate et orandis causis* ('distinguished for his nobility and his eloquent counsel'), and a dangerous tragedian, who chose death with his wife before condemnation, *ut dignum ueteribus Aemiliis* ('living up to the Aemilii of old', Tac. *Ann.* 6. 29. 4; cf. Sen. *Suas.* 2. 22; *stemma*, cf. Syme [1986] Table XVI).

187 So Virg. *Aen.* 6. 843f. lines up. . . *paruoque potentem* / ('powerful through dearth') with. . . *uel te, sulco, Serrane, serentem* / ('sowing seed when he was called to the consulship in 257 B.C. and. . . sowing seed now as he rises towards his earthly life', West 291): straightforward as a line of Virgil. The disguised Regulus drops out of the epic roll-call (Manil. *Astron.* 4. 148 has *Serranos Curiosque*). Sil. *Pun.* 6. 62–610 delays Fabius' emergence to cunctate by digressing to hear, with *Serranus, clarum nomen, tua, Regule, proles* ('S.—what a glorious name!—your offspring, Regulus'), his 'regal' father's praises sung, ready for fulminating Jove to veto Hannibal's march on Rome as Fabius emerges as underwhelming *rector* of Rome (vv. 589–618; 593).

188 So Plin. *Nat. Hist.* 11. 254, cf. Hor. *Serm.* 1. 3. 48, *illum* / *balbutit scaurum prauis fultum male talis* ('sweet-talks that character as "stout

ankles" when he's hopelessly propped up on bad ankle-bones'); cf. *LSJ s. v. skauros.*

189 'Delay' keeps Aeneas and us away from narrative time and event for the length of a whole book, for all the Sibyl's repeated abjurations of delay. It signifies text as resistance to over-crude teleological drive: find the stamina, but find the time to ask *your* questions. Otherwise the poet must be *your* dictatorial father-figure, no less.

190 The *nouus cos.* 146 did not use the triumphal title *Achaicus* assumed by his grandson (Syme [1986] 75).

191 Richardson (1942) reads Virgil as signalling grand quotation from Ennius in *magne Cato*. We hear no more than **Cossus'** bare name.

192 Ov. *Fast.* 2. 239, *puer impubes et adhuc non utilis armis* ('a growing boy still not expendable in combat). West (1993) 291 explains that these Fabian *Bandarlog* are tugging away little Maxim, who 'is not tired. He is dragging his feet on principle.' But they are *also* 'inspiring' *Fabius*— 'grabbing his imagination', the way that anyone, Fabius or not, gets 'carried away' by hearing their story, or stories (cf. Harries [1991] 161 and n. 62). And in the act, Virgil, Anchises, Maximus and we are all of us 'bodily transported' to the aspirational plane of patriotic myth. Silius treats the '300 Fabii' as amplificatory foil for *Cunctator* (*Pun.* 2. 3–6, 6. 637–9, 7. 39–61), but also, and as such, as anxiety-figure 'rivals' for fame: 7. 63f., *certauerit unus / ter centum armis* ('let one face three hundred in combat'). This was the idea in Virgil. The rhythms of *rapitis, Fabii. . . Maximus* brake down from *ill' es /* through *unus qui nobis cunctando* to stall in a complete halt at *rem. /*

193 Cf. Harries (1991) 158f.

194 Manil. *Astron.* 1. 790, / *inuictus mora Fabius* decocts the paradox, smart as ever: *Fabius* = undefeated through delaying tactics = invincible; he is set against a courtier's careful royal compliments: *uictorque. . . Liuius. . . Hasdrubalis socio. . . Nerone* ('Livius, conqueror of Hasdrubal through the cooperation of Nero') shows a quick, decisive, orthodox victory. Hasdrubal, *not* Hannibal, is defeated by prime Roman consular cooperation. . . Any Julio-Claudian can spot Livia Augusta's putative ancestor Liuius Salinator literally combining forces with Ti. Claudius Nero's forefather to produce triumph, just as the

Tiberian principate issues from the same 'marriage'. Yet Manilius also weaves the polar *exempla* into his race of Roman competitors up to the starry aether: all the starters have already qualified as winners, so they can all claim the prize, even the weird entrant Fabius, dawdling in a trance at the starting-gate in his alternative reality.

195 The famous tag is attributed to *Annales* 12 by Macrob. *Sat.* 6. 1. 23; that book was written in 172 (Varro *ap.* Gell. *Noct. Att.* 17. 21. 43), *about* the mid-190s: since Fabius died in 203, the context must have been a retrospect of some sort.

196 This last verse, apart from duly restoring. . . the verse to elegiacs, fuses together *qui* and *nobis*, and, since it refers to all chips off the old block who (must) emulate *Cunctator*, addresses not least 'his' Fabius Maximus, Paullus: what 'thing' might be restored to and by Paullus? What 'matter' should be 'put right' by him? What can he best rectify 'by hanging in there, sticking around, boring the opposition into submission'? What do these lines mean when read (written?) from Pontic exile?

197 See n. 84 for discussion of the montage of Ovid's passage.

198 The passage circles between the cue *magni. . . Iouis* ('great Jove') to the punchline *tanti cognominis* ('so great a title'). There is also a contiguity/connection between **Fabii** and (the ham-Republican) **Augustus**, who advertised that his adoptive Iulii had been enrolled in the 'Fabian' tribe on their arrival in Rome from Alba (Suet. *Aug.* 40. 2); Augustus also 'restored' the rites of the Luperci (*ib.* 31. 4, cf. Harries [1991] 150 n. 4).

199 Silius omits to say what became of Fabius, after Scipio shunted his counsel aside in *Punica* 16.

200 The MSS have: *noenum* (= 'at all'?).

201 Because. Because it's near O.

BIBLIOGRAPHY

WORKS REFERRED TO IN
THE TEXT AND NOTES

Standard commentaries are referred to by the author's name and are included in this Bibliography. Standard works of reference are abbreviated as follows: *CIL=Corpus Inscriptionum Latinarum*; *LSJ*=Liddell-Scott-Jones; *RE*=*Realencyclöpädie der Klassischen Altertumswissenshaft* ('Pauly-Wissowa'); *TLL*=*Thesaurus Linguae Latinae*: Journals are abbreviated as follows: *CQ=Classical Quarterly*: *PCPhS=Proceedings of the Cambridge Philological Society*; *JRS*=*Journal of Roman Studies*; *TAPhA*=Transactions of the American Philological Association; *SO=Symbolae Osloenses*; *JRA*=Journal of Roman Archaeology; *G&R=Greece and Rome*; *AJPh=American Journal of Philology*; *ZPE=Zeitschrift für Papyrologie and Epigraphik*; *HSPh=Harvard Studies in Classical Philology*; *LCM=Liverpool Classical Monthly*.

S. Bartsch (1994) *Actors in the Audience. Theatricality and Doublespeak from Nero to Hadrian* (Harvard)

M. Beagon (1992) *Roman Nature. The Thought of Pliny the Elder* (Oxford)

W. M. Bloomer (1992) *Valerius Maximus and the Rhetoric of the New Nobility* (London)

S. H. Braund (1981) 'Juvenal 8. 58–9', CQ 31. 221–3

S. H. Braund (1988) *Beyond Anger. A Study of Juvenal's Third Book of Satires* (Cambridge)

R. D. Brown (1991) '*Catonis nobile letum* and the List of Romans in Horace *Odes* 1. 12', *Phoenix* 45. 326–40

J. L. Butrica (1983) 'Propertius 3. 3. 7–12 and Ennius', CQ 33. 464–8

A. Degrassi (1937) *Inscriptiones Italiae* XIII. 3. *Elogia* (Rome)

C. H. Edwards (1993) *The Politics of Immorality in Ancient Rome* (Cambridge)

J. Elsner (1993) 'Seductions of Art: Encolpius and Eumolpus in a Neronian Picture Gallery', *PCPhS* 39. 30–47

D. C. Feeney (1986) 'History and Revelation in Vergil's Underworld', *PCPhS* 32. 1–24

D. P. Fowler (1991) 'Narrate and Describe: The Problem of Ekphrasis', *JRS* 81. 25–35

S. C. Fredericks (1971) 'Rhetoric and Morality in Juvenal's 8th Satire', *TAPhA* 102. 111–32

P. Gallivan (1992) 'The Nomenclature Patterns of the Roman Upper Class in the Early Empire: A Statistical Study', *Antichthon* 26. 51–79

C. Gnilka (1969) 'Eine typische Fehlerquelle der Juvenalinterpretation', *SO* 44. 90–108

S. Goldhill (1994) 'The Failure of Exemplarity', in *Modern Critical Theory and Classical Literature*, eds I. J. F. de Jong and J. P. Sullivan (Leiden) 51–73

E. Gowers (1993) 'Horace, *Satires* 1. 5: An Inconsequential Journey', *PCPhS* 39. 48–66

E. Gowers (1993A) *The Loaded Table. Representations of Food in Roman Literature* (Oxford)

A. P. Gregory (1994) '"Powerful Images": Responses to Portraits and the Political Uses of Images in Rome', *JRA* 7. 80–99

B. Harries (1991) 'Ovid and the *Fabii: Fasti* 2. 193–474', CQ 41. 150–68

J. Henderson (1988) 'Entertaining Arguments: Terence *Adelphoe*', in *Post-Structuralist Classics*, ed. A. Benjamin (London) 192–226

BIBLIOGRAPHY

J. Henderson (1989) 'Satire Writes "Woman": Gendersong', PCPhS
215. 50–80

J. Henderson (1995) 'Pump Up the Volume: Juvenal Satire I. 1–21',
PCPhS 41. 101–37

H. Hine (1987) 'Aeneas and the Arts (Vergil, Aeneid 6. 847–50)', in
Homo Viator, Classical Essays for John Bramble, eds M. Whitby, P.
Hardie and M. Whitby (Bristol) 173–83

D. Jackson (1987) 'Verism and the Ancestral Portrait', G&R 34. 32–47

H. D. Jocelyn (1993), ed. Tria Lustra, Essays and Notes Presented to
John Pinsent (Liverpool Classical Papers 3)

W. Kierdorf (1994) 'CECINIT oder CECINI? Neue berlegungen zum
Text von Properz 3, 3, 7', Hermes 122.3 68–72

D. E. E. Kleiner (1992) Roman Sculpture (Yale)

R. LaFleur (1972) 'A Note on Juvenal, 10, 201f.', AJPh 93. 598–600

J. Linderski (1990) 'The Surname of M. Antonius Creticus and the
Cognomina ex Victis Gentibus', ZPE 80. 159–64

H. W. Litchfield (1914) 'National Exempla Virtutis in Roman Literatu-
re', HSPh 25. 1–71

E. S. McCartney (1912) Figurative Uses of Animal Names in Latin and
their Application to Military Devices (Pennsylvania)

R. Maltby (1991) A Lexicon of Ancient Latin Etymologies (Leeds)

R. G. Mayer (1991) 'Roman Historical Exempla in Seneca', in Sénèque
et la Prose Latine, Entretiens Fondation Hardt, ed. P. Grimal, 36.
141–76

Y. Nadeau (1985) 'Traduction and Censors (Juvenal 2. 159; 8. 17; 7.
16; 11. 31: Virgil, A. 6. 697ff.)', LCM 10. 44–8

R. G. M. Nisbet (1962) Review of Clausen (Oxford Classical Text, first
edition), JRS 52. 233–8

A. J. Pomeroy (1988) 'Livy's Death Notices', G&R 35. 172–83

W. J. Raschke (1990) 'The virtue of Lucilius', Latomus 49. 352–69

E. Rawson (1985) Intellectual Life in the Roman Republic (London)

L. J. D. Richardson (1942) 'Direct Citation of Ennius in Virgil', CQ 36.
40–2

O. Salomies (1992) Adoptive and Polyonomous Nomenclature in the
Roman Empire (Helsinki)

165

B. Salway (1994) 'What's in a Name? A Survey of Roman Onomastic Patterns from *c.* 700 B.C. to A.D. 700', *JRS* 84. 124–45

O. Skutsch (1968) *Studia Enniana* (Oxford)

J. E. Skydsgaard (1992) 'Varro's *De Imaginibus* and Ancient Portraiture: A Note', in *Ancient Portraiture: Image and Message*, eds T. Fischer-Hansen, J. Lund, M. Nielsen, A. Rathje (Copenhagen. *Acta Hyperborea* 4)

R. Syme (1958) 'Imperator Caesar. A Study in Nomenclature', *Historia* 7. 172–88

R. Syme (1958A) *Tacitus* (Oxford)

R. Syme (1960) 'Piso Frugi and Crassus Frugi', *JRS* 50. 12–20

R. Syme (1978) *History in Ovid* (Oxford)

R. Syme (1982) 'The Marriage of Rubellius Blandus', *AJPh* 103. 62–85

R. Syme (1986) *The Augustan Aristocracy* (Oxford)

D. West (1993) 'The Pageant of the Heroes as Panegyric (VIRGIL, *AEN.* 6. 760–886)', in Jocelyn (1993) 283–96

M. Wilson (1993) 'Silius' *Punica*', in *Roman Epic*, ed. A. J. Boyle (London) 218–36

T. P. Wiseman (1970) 'Pulcher Claudius', *HSPh* 74. 207–21

T. P. Wiseman (1971) *New Men in the Roman Senate, 139* B.C. – A.D. 14 (Oxford)

T. P. Wiseman (1985) 'Competition and Cooperation', in *Roman Political Life, 90* B.C. – A.D. 69 (*Exeter Studies in History* 7) 3–19

T. P. Wiseman (1993) 'Rome and the Resplendent Aemilii', in Jocelyn (1993) 181–92

P. Zanker (1988) *The Power of Images in the Age of Augustus* (Michigan)

INDEX

CHIEF PASSAGES DISCUSSED IN THE TEXT AND NOTES

Cicero, *Ad Atticum* 6. 1. 25: n. 79

Elogium of Fabius Maximus (Degrassi nos. 14 + 80): 52, n. 87

Ennius, *Annales* 363 Skutsch: 129, n. 200

Horace, *Odes* 1. 12: 29–32, nn. 39, 40, 71, Appendix 1:97–114; 4.1–2: n. 88

Juvenal 1. 108: n. 61; 7: 94–6, n.172; 9: 96, n.174

Livy: 5. 46. 2f. : 57; 24. 44. 9: 54; 30. 26. 8: 148; 30. 26. 9: 129; 30. 45. 7: 37

Lucan 2. 234: n. 31; 3.514: n. 31; 5. 16–30: n. 26; 6. 785–7: 47, n. 159; 786: n. 50; 788: n. 48; 789f. : n. 56; 792f. : n. 180; 793f. : nn.157–8, n. 180; 795f. : n. 132, n. 155

Manilius 1. 778–81: n. 161; 778: n. 180; 782f. : n. 57; 783: n. 143; 784f. : n. 183; 787: 45; 789: n. 56; 790: n. 194; 791: n. 132; 792: n. 48; 794f.: n. 157; 795f. : n.78; 797f. : n. 182

Ovid, *Amores* 1. 8. 65f. : 60

Ovid, *Ars Amatoria* 3. 409f. : n. 53

Ovid, *Ex Ponto* 3. 6: n. 27; 4. 3. 41: n. 56; 4. 12: 38

Ovid, *Fasti* 1. 587–616: Appendix 3:126–8; 594: n. 140; 596: 48; 2.195–452: n. 84; 195–242: 55, n. 103; 225: 56, n. 104; 239: n. 192; 240: n. 118; 241f. : 125

Propertius 3. 3. 7f. : n. 52

Silius 1. 676–9: n. 26; 693: n. 81; 2. 8–10: n. 150; 3. 592–629: n. 37; 4.

192–215: n. 28; 495–7, 515: n. 155; 5. 77–9, 121f. : n. 57; 231–4: n. 26; 6. 62–610: n. 187; 7. 1: n. 118; 20: n. 81; 63f. : n. 192; 539–65: 55; 8. 298, 306: n. 128; 463ff., 469ff. : n. 65; 10. 194–201: n. 65; 260–91: n. 26; 305–8: n. 128; 12. 278f.: n. 184; 13. 231–3: n. 158; 721f. : n. 181; 722f. : 38; 724–8: n. 161; 853–93: n. 158; 15. 337f. : n. 184; 17. 619–27: 38; 645: n. 54

Tabula Lugdunensis col. II. 24f. : 53

Tacitus, *Annals* 2. 32. 1: n. 41; 3. 48: n. 28; 3. 76. 4f. : n. 41; 11. 24. 1: n. 140; 12. 24. 1: n. 107; 15. 41. 1: n. 107

Valerius Maximus 5. 8. 3: 45, n. 69

Virgil, *Aeneid* 6. 754f. : 30; 756–886: 106, Appendix 2: 115–22; 808–12: n. 177; 811: n. 37; 818–23: n. 162; 824f. : nn. 105, 132, 158; 825: n. 50; 826–46: 124; 837–9: 36; 841: 67, n. 129, 108; 842: n. 155; 842f.: n. 48; 843: 58; 843f. : 45, n. 187; 845f.: 45; 847f.: 17, n. 15; 849–53: n. 15; 8.535: n. 149; 650f.: n. 161; 724: n. 147

Virgil, *Georgic* 1. 169–72: n. 50; 169: n. 105

[Virgil] *Culex* 358–71: n. 105; 361: nn. 159, 161; 365: n. 161; 366: 38